Happy Steeping!

STEEPED

RECIPES INFUSED WITH TEA

annelies zijderveld

Photographs by Stephanie Shih

**Andrews McMeel
Publishing®**

Kansas City · Sydney · London

for my parents, Hendrik and Mary Lou

There are those who love to get dirty
and fix things.
They drink coffee at dawn,
beer after work,

And those who stay clean,
just appreciate things,
At breakfast they have milk
and juice at night.

There are those who do both,
they drink tea.

—GARY SNYDER

CONTENTS

DEAR READER,

I never anticipated getting so deeply steeped in tea. Now, I can't imagine what life would look like otherwise. The story begins in a kitchen, as most good stories do. A few weeks before I would receive my master's degree in inter-cultural studies, with the intent of moving to India, I was stirring a pot of soup in the dormitory kitchen when my friend Sandra sauntered in, frazzled from being short-handed at work—at a tea company. As she described the help they needed, I asked the fateful question: "Where do I apply?"

Thus began my foray into the field of tea. What started as a summer stint at Mighty Leaf Tea, then a small company of nine employees, kept my tea curiosity clinched for almost eight years. One afternoon, I reached for a pinch of lustrous Japanese green tea. Those crunchy, long bluish-green tea leaves begged to be baked into crumbly buttery cookies. I began to see the potential of using tea as a spice, rather than only a drink.

This is a book I have been writing in my head for fourteen years, spurred by ongoing experimentation in the fascinating ways tea can be infused into everyday foods. All these years later, tea is still astounding me with its resilience and possibilities. I'm thrilled you've joined in the journey and relish passing the infuser on.

Warmly,

annelies

TEA PRIMER

The myth of tea's origins is as interesting as all of the variations of the leaf. In 2737 BC, Shen Nung sat underneath a tree contemplating philosophy and holding a cup of hot water in his hands. From the tree above, a leaf floated down. Shen Nung sipped the infusion, astounded. No matter how it actually happened, it only fits that the father of Chinese medicine should be said to have discovered tea, given its health attributes.

Some of the most unforgettable conversations in literature are exchanged over teacups. Between riddles, the mad hatter argues with Alice in Wonderland that "It's always teatime." When Mr. Tumnus meets Lucy in *The Lion, the Witch and the Wardrobe*, he invites her to tea and toast. It is at teatime that Anne of Green Gables mistakes currant wine for raspberry cordial, accidentally getting her best friend Diana Barry drunk. At Lowood school, Jane Eyre has to fend for herself at teatime.

Teatime harbors an unexpected secret in Thomas Hardy's "At Tea." Tea appears four times in T. S. Eliot's "The Love Song of J. Alfred Prufrock," with the title character paralyzed by what could happen "[b]efore the taking of a toast and tea." And it is at teatime that Mrs. Manresa distracts herself in Virginia Woolf's last novel, *Between the Acts*. C. S. Lewis declared that no book or cup of tea existed large enough to quench his thirst. While in boarding school at King Edward's, J.R.R. Tolkien and four classmates formed a coterie called the Tea Club.

Beyond literature, the musician Moby founded and co-owned the popular New York City teahouse Teany. Supermodel Miranda Kerr, an avid tea drinker, has partnered with Royal Albert to create her own teapot and teacup collection. Benedict Cumberbatch issued an invitation to fellow Sherlock Holmes portrayers Jonny Lee Miller and Robert Downey, Jr., to meet up over tea and share notes on the character. In *Star Trek: The Next Generation*, Patrick Stewart's Captain Jean-Luc Picard's usual order from his ready room's replicator is "tea, Earl Grey, hot." And tea lover Oprah Winfrey has created her own chai blend with Teavana and purportedly travels with her own loose tea accessories.

THE CHAMELEON:
Camellia Sinensis

What exactly is tea? Whether black, oolong, green, white, or Pu-erh, all teas come from the same *Camellia sinensis* plant. From there, the nuances of cultivation and processing determine the final tea you drink. From field to cup involves several stages. Tea leaves are hand-plucked or gathered by machine—each "leaf" properly composed of two leaves and a bud. Then they are sorted, cleaned, and spread on racks or bamboo trays to wither for up to twenty-four hours, making them soft and pliable. In the next stage the leaves are rolled or tossed, and in the case of Chinese green teas,

Pensive they sit, and roll their languid eyes,
nibble their toast, and cool their tea with sighs
— JOHN KEATS

even pan-fried, the goal during this stage being to bruise the leaves to break down their cellular structure and start the enzymatic process that draws out tannins and begins oxidation.

How long the leaves oxidize determines the type of tea produced. Black teas oxidize the longest, producing the most caffeinated teas with a bolder, astringent flavor. Oolong teas oxidize somewhere between black and green teas, making some oolongs closer in caffeine and flavor profile to black teas and others to green. Green teas have little to no oxidizing time and therefore less caffeine with a mellower flavor ranging from nutty or vegetal to floral or fruity. White teas skip oxidation altogether, giving them the least caffeine and mildest flavor. And in a further variation, Pu-erh teas are heaped into a pile to ferment and age like wine, yielding a caffeine level close to black tea and incredibly earthy, malty notes that can be reminiscent of dark, thick stout. Pu-erh teas are drunk after rich meals to aid digestion.

The next stage stops oxidation through steaming or pan-firing. Leaves are rolled by hand for specialty and whole leaf teas— the ones that command premium prices.

A note on herbal teas: Herbal "tea" is technically a misnomer, since no *Camellia sinensis* is involved. Instead, they are more accurately called herbal blends, infusions, or tisanes. If you are avoiding caffeine but miss the flavor of tea, try rooibos, which is available in many flavors including Earl Grey and chai. Personally, I'm

not a fan of decaffeinated teas, which taste more like whatever is flavoring them and lack astringency. For cooking purposes, I suggest sticking with the recipes using herbal tisanes.

Terroir

Camellia sinensis can be grown in many environments, from shady mountainside to out under the stare of a surly sun. What is remarkable is that Darjeeling tea from the Lesser Himalayan mountains of northern India displays much different qualities than Ceylon tea from tropical Sri Lanka. Whereas Darjeeling, the Champagne of the tea world (literally, only teas from the Darjeeling region of India can be thus named, akin to Champagne appellations), have high floral notes, some astringency, and a delicate flavor with muscatel notes, Ceylon teas have smooth honey notes and brew terrific iced tea. The climate and geography differences account for their varied flavor profiles.

In other words, tea, like coffee or wine, evokes *terroir*. The very place of its cultivation affects and changes the plant's structure, yielding differing final outcomes of the same species.

At First Flush: Seasonality

You might come across the word "flush" on tea labels. It is a denotation of the season in which the leaves were picked. First flush teas are typically picked in early spring and exhibit a more aromatic, milder flavor. Second flush teas are usually picked between May and June and offer a more robust flavor, making them a popular choice. Then there's silver needle, a stunning white tea that is hand-picked during a very limited time period that can be as little as a forty-eight–hour window each year and brews a delicate ivory-colored tea.

TEA CULTURE

While tea is popular around the world, the ways it is consumed vary considerably. In Russia, they might stir a spoonful of jam into smoky, stiff black tea. In Morocco, they drink a bracingly sweet green tea edged with fresh mint leaves. The most popular teas in China—Dragon Well, tieguanyin, and Pu-erh—are little known here. Taiwan is known for highly floral and exquisite Formosa oolongs. In Japan, the tea ceremony is centered around the brewing of matcha. India likes its tea milky, spiced, and sometimes sweet. In the United Kingdom, tea is typically served black and assertive, with milk or lemon. And 85 percent of tea drunk in the United States is iced, according to the Tea Association of the U.S.A.

TEA COOKING

The idea for *Steeped* started with a question: What would it look like to invite tea into every meal of the day? What if tea, with its call to slow down and smell the (jasmine) flowers, marked every day with moments in which to luxuriate in living? It seems too delicious an idea, in our busy times, not to pursue. Let's get brewing!

TEA COOKING CABINET

While there are as many tea blends as the imagination can create, in *Steeped* we use ten classic teas readily available at your favorite teahouse, specialty grocer, or natural food store.

BLACK TEAS
English Breakfast

Stout and sturdy, English breakfast is built to last. No one black tea makes up an English breakfast, and even the leaf size can vary by purveyor. Smaller leaves brew more quickly (good for iced tea) and offer a stronger cup. My Dutch-Bolivian dad, the original tea drinker in our family, who toted around a bottomless glass of iced tea, taught me to appreciate strong astringent black tea. English breakfast incorporates into desserts well, especially with brown sugar to draw out the caramel notes. It also tastes incredible paired with citrus.

Earl Grey

Earl Grey consists of black tea scented with the oil of the citrus fruit bergamot, which flaunts a slightly bitter flavor somewhere between lemon and orange. From there, though, come deviations. Is the black tea Indian, Chinese, or Sri Lankan? Is the bergamot artificial or first-pressed oil from Calabria? Earl Grey pairs well with chocolate, dairy sweets, stone fruits, carrots, and other vegetables.

Lapsang Souchong

If you only add one tea to your kitchen, let lapsang souchong be it. This Chinese black tea is smoked over fir tree root, imparting a campfire smokiness. It is the single most useful cooking-with-tea ingredient for its ability to work overtime. Beware—a little goes a long way. Lapsang souchong pairs well with fungi and root vegetables and brings something unexpected to sweets.

Masala Chai

I first experienced this now-popular Indian spiced tea while visiting a friend in Delhi. Her version added fresh ginger to inexpensive black tea granules, milk, and sugar. Some people add more cardamom, others more cinnamon. Star anise, cloves, or pepper might be included. Chai pairs well with fall fruit and chocolate.

GREEN TEAS
Dragon Well

Also known as *lung ching*, this pan-fried Chinese green tea is what I think of when I think of green tea. It is one of China's most famous, which is saying a lot since so many teas—in fact, most of the tea consumed worldwide—come from China. Telltale signs of Dragon Well include long, flattened leaves. Dragon Well boasts a superb nutty flavor profile and complexity that make it a darling of the tea cook's kitchen and pair magnificently with vegetables and savory dishes.

Jasmine

This blend reads like a romance novel—jasmine blossoms sandwiched between layers of green tea leaves. The jasmine envelops the tea with floral essence, lush aroma, and distinctive flavor. Jasmine may be more mellow and refined than bolder teas, but it quietly asserts itself with melon, bittersweet chocolate, and citrus.

Moroccan Mint

In Morocco, Chinese gunpowder green tea is blended with mint. The version from Rishi Tea uses peppermint for a bright, open flavor. Other blends use spearmint for a more mellow profile. One of my favorites, Marrakesh mint from Mighty Leaf Tea, uses nana mint, a subdued Moroccan mint reminiscent of chocolate mint. Lemongrass is added to others, such as those from Choice Organic Teas, Allegro Coffee & Tea, and Tazo. Sipping the wide range of offerings can be a fascinating process, perfect for a tasting party. Moroccan mint green tea pairs well with savory and sweet recipes alike.

Matcha

Japanese matcha takes the prize for most exceptional tea. The flavor is grassy and stark. What you are looking for in a fine, high-quality matcha is the bright green of Technicolor grass. Once you try it, it is near to impossible to go back to subpar matcha that is dull in color and taste. Tencha leaves, the same tea leaves used to make gyokuro, one of the most exquisite (and expensive) teas, are stone-ground into matcha powder. Matcha is beloved by chefs for seamlessly integrating its exotic flair and playful color into savory and sweet recipes alike.

HERBAL TISANES

So many herbal tisanes exist that it is impossible to whittle down the options to a workable list, but two stand apart for their versatility and ability to incorporate into everyday foods.

Chamomile

When I was growing up, my Mexican mom would bring me a steaming cup of *manzanilla*, as chamomile is called in Spanish, to help me sleep. Then again, she would offer it to me with a stir of honey when I was feeling sick, too. Chamomile's highly floral aroma and honey-like flavor are as distinctive as its dried yellow flowers and pair well with honey, corn, bananas, and dairy.

Rooibos

Rooibos is often called "red tea," although technically no tea is present in it. Rooibos means "red bush" and hails from South Africa, where the needle-like leaves are harvested from the *Aspalathus linearis* shrub. Of all tisanes, it tastes closest to black tea and is a good choice for people who like tea but avoid caffeine. Rooibos pairs well with carrots, pumpkin, vanilla, citrus, and berries.

METHODS *for* COOKING *with* TEA

While professional chefs have been employing tea as an ingredient for some time, my intent in *Steeped* is to give practical ways to add tea to your everyday cooking in the home kitchen.

Ground Tea

Grinding leaves into powder in a spice grinder or mortar and pestle exploits the true flavor of tea, especially in dishes such as Berta's Egg Salad Sandwiches (page 45) or Butternut Squash Hash (page 28).

Tea Spice Blends

Think of tea as a spice, and keep your spice grinder handy. Make your own Arnold Palmer Powder (page 6) or Tea Furikake (page 54).

Brewed Tea

Using brewed tea instead of water or other liquids in a recipe gives unexpected pizzazz, as in the Smoky Tomato Soup with Parmesan Thyme Crisps (page 65).

Hot Tea Infusions

Hot infusions are a reliable quick way to incorporate tea into dairy, as in Chocolate Earl Grey Custard (page 105).

Cold Tea Infusions

Cold infusions are ideal for probiotic-rich ingredients whose live cultures would be killed by heat, as in the Tea Crackers with Herbed Labneh (page 55).

Poaching in Tea

Portobello Steak Frites (page 74) and Earl Grey Poached Pears (page 90) gain a lot of flavor in a short time by cooking in brewed tea.

TEA BREWING MECHANICS
How to Select Tea

Just because a tea is expensive does not make it the best. Determine how you want to use the tea to decide what kind to purchase. While you can stock your tea shelves with only whole leaf teas, you can also buy their broken leaf counterparts called fannings or tea dust. I have learned to appreciate these also, as they brew quickly and make a more astringent cup of tea. They're especially satisfactory for iced tea (think Lipton tea bags—my dad's go-to).

Whole leaf teas harness a better brew; this is true. Full, lustrous intact tea leaves provide the best experience and are also purported to hold greater health benefits. Green tea is in the superfoods pantheon, celebrated for its high antioxidant content of polyphenols and L-theanine, an amino acid.

Organic Offerings

Because we are cooking with tea, the lion's share of teas used in *Steeped* are organic. Organic options have steadily increased, making them easier to find in stores or online.

How to Store Tea

The enemies of tea are light, air, and moisture. While glass containers let you see the beautiful leaves, they are not practical for keeping tea long-term. If you do use glass containers, keep them in a dark place. In a cool, dark cabinet away from the stove, tea can last a year or more.

Brewing Tea for Cooking

All the hot tea instructions that follow are for a single serving to be used in cooking, steeped in whatever vessel is convenient: a teapot, cup, or bowl. Put the leaves in your vessel. Use an infuser, or strain after the tea is done steeping. Pour the water over in a swirling motion. After steeping, strain immediately through a strainer or a fine-mesh sieve into another bowl. The amount of liquid trapped in the leaves can be significant enough to change the results of your recipe, so press on the leaves or bag to extract all the steeped liquid; discard the leaves or bag.

BLACK TEA

Tea: 1 teaspoon or 2½ grams of loose leaves
Water: 12 ounces of near-boiling or boiling (208°F to 212°F)
Steep time: 4 minutes

GREEN TEA

Tea: 1 tablespoon of loose leaves
Water: 12 ounces of 170°F to 180°F
Steep time: 2 to 3 minutes

OOLONG TEA

Brewing oolong tea is quite unique: The first steeping is considered an awakening of the leaves. The tea is not usually drunk until the third or fourth steeping. For cooking, use the following method:
Tea: 1 teaspoon of loose leaves
Water: 12 ounces of 190°F
Steep time: 4 minutes

HERBAL TISANE

Since tisanes contain no tannin, they can be brewed hotter and longer. The infusions will become stronger, not bitter.
Tea: 1 tablespoon of loose leaves or blossoms
Water: 12 ounces of 212°F
Steep time: 5 minutes (the typical brew time for drinking) or longer, if you want more flavor, especially for cooking purposes

ICED TEA

To make iced tea, you will first make a concentrate that is diluted with water and ice.
Tea: 3 tablespoons of English breakfast loose tea leaves
Water: 16 ounces boiling
Steep time: 4 minutes
Strain the tea through a fine-mesh sieve into a pitcher. Press on the leaves to extract all the steeped liquid; discard the leaves. Pour 16 ounces cold water into the pitcher, stir in 8 ounces (1 cup) of ice cubes, and refrigerate. Serve unsweetened or sweeten to taste.

TEA MILK

Bring 24 ounces of milk to almost boiling at 190°F over medium heat, stirring so it does not burn. Turn off the heat. Sprinkle 3 teaspoons of loose tea into a large bowl. Pour the hot milk over the leaves in a swirling motion. Steep for 5 minutes. Strain using a fine-mesh sieve. Press on the leaves to extract all the steeped liquid. Use hot or cool and refrigerate. Sweeten to taste.

SPA TEA

Move over cold-brewed coffee. Cold-brewed tea—also known as spa tea—is a refreshing, milder brew. Pour 24 ounces of water into a pitcher. Stir in 3 tablespoons of loose or 6 bags tea. Add fresh herbs and sliced fruit—I like strawberries and lemon. Refrigerate to infuse overnight. To serve, remove the tea bags or strain through a sieve if using loose tea. Remember to press on the bags or leaves to extract all steeped liquid.

Loose Tea vs. Bagged Tea

Tea bags were a nifty invention allowing easier brewing without the gadgetry required for loose tea. Still, loose tea is preferable, and a teapot with a built-in infuser makes loose tea almost as convenient. Practically speaking, loose tea is cheaper: Consider that a 4-ounce container of English breakfast tea yields fifty-five total 1 teaspoon servings versus a box of fifteen or twenty tea bags, which yields only that number of servings. If you do use tea bags, look for certified organic tea companies to ensure paper bags that have not been sprayed and are non-GMO compliant.

The recipes that follow give loose or bagged tea options with each recipe, except when it's more practical to go with one or the other. I have kept cost constraints and consumption size in mind. Many tea bags are filled with a ½ tablespoon of tea, but this can vary by manufacturer and tea type. So if you are substituting tea bags for loose tea in a recipe, simply measure out the tea from the tea bag.

"Your tea is to your mind, I hope"—
"Exceeding good"—
"Pray one more cup."
"Your toast is very nice; I've eat Till I'm asham'd."
—FRANCIS FAWKES

COOKING-*with*-TEA TOOLS

Wide-Mouth Fine-Mesh Sieve

For cooking purposes, a sieve might just be the perfect brewing apparatus for loose tea. Pair it with a large nonreactive bowl, and you're set. Look for a sieve with fine holes so smaller leaves don't fall through.

Electric Kettle with Variable Temperature Settings

This one is a splurge, but worthwhile for both tea cook and avid tea drinker. It frees you up to not keep a thermometer and yet not scorch delicate tea leaves, as with a one-temperature pot. Variable temperature kettles allow you to select what type of tea you are brewing (and often include a French Press button for you coffee drinkers—I know this is a tea book, but I won't tell if you swing both ways). If you drink a lot of tea or plan to be cooking quite a bit with tea, there are larger models from Japan that get the job done especially well.

Stovetop Kettle

I never anted up and bought a fancy stovetop tea kettle, though if that's your cuppa, just make sure to heat your tea under boiling for green and white teas.

Thermometer

It might be an extra step to test your water temperature, but your tea drinking and cooking experience will be the better for it. A green tea brewed at 190°F or 212°F scalds the tender leaves, leaving them bitter and astringent. Humor me and try measuring the water temperature. You may be astonished by the difference.

Timer

Where would we be in tea brewing without a timer? Thankfully, smartphones and microwaves come equipped with timers.

Proper Teapot

I can't help myself using the word "proper" if only to underscore the importance of finding a teapot that suits your needs. So many styles exist! In China, *yi xing* teapots made of clay take on the flavor attributes of the tea to such a degree that sometimes people have one teapot for black tea and another for green tea. Japan's stunning and heavy cast-iron *tetsubin* teapots go from stovetop to trivet with ease. In Morocco they use flat-bottomed steel teapots with plastic handles. Around the Middle East, eastern Europe, and Russia, large metal water urns called samovars feature a flat top surface on which a teapot of tea concentrate can keep heated before being diluted with boiling water from the urn.

There is a teapot out there for each experience you can imagine. I would only stipulate that if a teapot comes with a strainer, make sure the strainer is fine-gauge enough to capture small leaves. For most *Steeped* recipes, I recommend the bowl and sieve approach in brewing tea for cooking (page xxiii). I reserve teapots primarily for drinking.

Cup-Sized Strainers

I have often said that I am like loose tea: I need a lot of space to unfurl. Many kinds of infusers vie for your attention and pocketbook. There is only one type you should look for and the others might as well be consigned to the trash heap. That statement may seem harsh, but nothing holds quality loose tea leaves back from unfurling like a tiny tea ball or slender infuser stick. This area is one on which I am most vehement. If you're going to spend the money for beautiful loose teas, purchase a sturdy infuser with a wide enough mouth or one that is deep enough to give those leaves space to unfurl. You want as much surface area of the leaves to come in contact with the water as possible. As with strainers, look for a fine-gauge knit to ensure capturing tiny leaves.

Tea Pitchers

Use a sturdy glass pitcher when brewing iced tea. Plastic pitchers retain flavors. If making iced tea from loose tea leaves, I recommend the bowl and sieve approach, then straining the brew into the pitcher.

Spice Grinder

With the help of a powerhouse spice grinder, you can grind any tea leaves into coarse powder or powder almost as fine as matcha. If you do not own a spice grinder, use a mortar and pestle. In our house, we have two grinders: the coffee grinder and the-everything-else grinder. Can I nudge you to not use your coffee grinder to grind tea unless you want coffee-flavored tea powder?

Tea Whisk

Matcha green tea powder is about as finely ground as you can get. To incorporate it into custards, hot beverages, and such, a whisk is imperative. Tea whisks made of bamboo can be found in most tea shops and some natural grocery stores. For *Steeped* recipes, a sturdy regular whisk and arm power suffice.

Special Kitchen Tools

CHEESECLOTH *and* NUT-MILK BAG

Cheesecloth is useful for making the Buddha Hand Rooibos Marmalade (page 22), and the finer-gauge nut-milk bag works marvelously for making the Pistachio Panna Cotta (page 103).

BLENDER

All *Steeped* blended recipes were developed with a high-speed blender in mind. If you do not have one, simply blend until smooth and then strain through a fine-mesh sieve.

FOOD SCALE

Weighing flour can make such a big difference in baked goods. I find it to be the easiest and most precise way to bake; however, I am mindful that it is not the only way. As such, you will also find cup equivalents.

A *STEEPED* STOCKED KITCHEN: *Regular Rotation Ingredients*

Olive Oil

Olive oil is my go-to when heating food at low temperatures or imparting its flavors (Peppery! Fruity! Floral!) into the dish in question.

Safflower Oil or Grapeseed Oil

For heating foods at high temperatures, I reach for one of these two oils, which have higher smoke points and neutral flavors.

Kosher Salt

These recipes are made with kosher salt, which I prefer for its versatility and mildness. If you use sea salt, adjust the recipes to taste.

Spelt Flour

If you have ever considered whole grain flours, start with spelt. This ancient grain imparts nuttiness and a toothsome quality without being overly sturdy or heavy. It can even often be swapped in for all-purpose flour. You will find that most of the baked recipes in this book include spelt flour. If you choose to bypass the spelt, simply use all-purpose flour, but it is my promise that if you buy one bag of spelt flour, I will show you how to bake through it.

Eggs

For all the recipes that call for eggs, I use large organic, free-range eggs.

Whole Milk Dairy

Did you know that whole milk dairy is less processed than low-fat versions? It is another reason, along with richer, more full-bodied flavor, that I reach for whole milk or plain whole milk yogurt. If you skimp somewhere, don't let it be dairy.

COOKING THROUGH *the* BOOK

Of course I hope you read the book with a cup of tea in hand. If you have a favorite tea or your tea pantry is already jammed full, you may want to visit the Recipes by Tea & Tisane index on page 114 and cook through your collection. However you begin, loop me in on Twitter or Instagram at @anneliesz with the tag #SteepedBook or search for me on Pinterest as anneliesz—I'd love to follow your tea-cooking adventures!

drinking tea alone—
every day the butterfly
stops by

—KOBAYASHI ISSA

MORNING TEA

BAKED

Blueberry Scones with Rooibos Honey Butter

Green Tea Granola

Arnold Palmer Poppy Seed Muffins

Sally's Masala Chai Pumpkin Bread

COMFORT

Masala Chai Applesauce

Cranberry-Coconut Rooibos Oat Porridge

COLD

Earl Grey Yogurt Parfaits

Matcha Chia Pudding Parfaits

Blueberry Black Tea Smoothie

Ginger-Mango Green Tea Smoothie

Chamomile Lassi

PRESERVES

Sweet Tea Jelly

Strawberry Chamomile Jam

Buddha's Hand Rooibos Marmalade

Now through lace curtains I can see
the huge Wolf Moon going down,
and soon the sky will lighten, turning
first gray, then pink, then blue. . . .

—JANE KENYON

Mornings come whether we pull the covers over our heads or fling off the sheets eager to slip into another day. For many, the ritual of a pot set over high flame or an electric kettle skittering as if trying to contain excitement starts our days. The cupboard is thrown open. A favorite mug is retrieved. Fingernails slide under a tightly capped tin lid. A paper pouch is torn in one clean strip. We have begun waking up. As water swirls over the leaves, the drifting aroma begins to ground us. The day is yours to seize as you please.

BLUEBERRY SCONES *with* ROOIBOS HONEY BUTTER

This rooibos honey butter melts into terra-cotta pools of sweetness on warm scones. Pulverize the rooibos leaves with a spice grinder, or cut open a bag of Republic of Tea's Organic Double Red Rooibos.

BLUEBERRY SCONES

1½ cups (210 grams) all-purpose flour

½ teaspoon kosher salt

3 tablespoons sugar

2 teaspoons baking powder

8 tablespoons unsalted butter, cubed and chilled

¾ cup plus 1 tablespoon buttermilk

¼ cup blueberries

ROOIBOS HONEY BUTTER

8 tablespoons unsalted butter, room temperature

¾ teaspoon finely ground rooibos

2 teaspoons raw honey

MAKES 5 TO 6 SCONES

TO MAKE THE SCONES: Preheat the oven to 350°F. Lightly flour a work surface.

Whisk the flour, salt, sugar, and baking powder in a mixing bowl. Cut in the butter using a pastry cutter or two knives until the chunks are pea-sized. Pour the buttermilk into the bowl and combine until shaggy.

Gather the dough into a ball and place it on the floured work surface. Gently fold in one-third of the blueberries at a time until all the blueberries have been integrated. Flour a rolling pin and press down lightly from the middle, rolling away from you and rotating the dough. Roll and rotate until the dough is 1 inch thick.

Flour a biscuit cutter and cut the scones close together— make sure to press all the way down. Gather the scraps, roll, and cut out the rest—you should get five or six scones.

Place them 1 inch apart on a 13 by 9-inch sheet pan. Bake 20 minutes, or until lightly browned.

TO MAKE THE BUTTER: In a small bowl, stir the butter, finely ground rooibos, and honey until combined and the color of the dust on Mars. Use at room temperature or refrigerate until use (for pats, roll the butter into a log in a sheet of parchment paper and chill until hard).

GREEN TEA GRANOLA

I serve these with lychee chunks, crisp Asian pear, and labneh, with a wake-up grating of fresh ginger to pull it all together. You can make your own labneh, or use store-bought (my favorite brand is Karoun), or Greek yogurt instead.

GREEN TEA GRANOLA

4 cups rolled oats

2 cups chopped walnuts

¼ cup sesame seeds

4 teaspoons amaranth

2 tablespoons loose or 4 bags (cut open) Dragon Well green tea

6 tablespoons safflower, grapeseed, or other neutral oil

4 tablespoons maple syrup

¼ teaspoon ground cardamom

½ teaspoon kosher salt

1 cup golden raisins

MAKES 2 QUARTS GRANOLA

PREHEAT THE OVEN TO 275°F. Place a sheet of parchment paper onto an 18-inch sheet pan. Stir together the oats, walnuts, and sesame seeds in a medium bowl.

Heat a small fry pan over medium-high heat until a drop of water sizzles. Pour in ½ teaspoon amaranth, cover, and pop like popcorn for 30 seconds or until popping slows. Listen carefully! Amaranth pops quickly and will burn just as fast. Move the popped amaranth from the pan to the bowl and repeat with the remaining amaranth, ½ teaspoon at a time.

In a small saucepan set over low heat, combine the tea, oil, maple syrup, cardamom, and salt. Stir until heated through and combined. Stir the tea and oil into the oats to coat.

Pour the green tea granola onto the baking sheet, spreading evenly in a single layer. Bake for 32 minutes or until golden brown, stirring three times or every 8 minutes. Cool the granola to harden on the baking sheet and stir in the raisins.

the State
remained in
resignation as
commented on
affairs as an

ARNOLD PALMER POPPY SEED MUFFINS

Calling lemon lovers! You may never send a lemon peel to the compost bin again. Arnold Palmer powder is also wonderful on gingersnaps or over oatmeal.

ARNOLD PALMER POWDER

1 tablespoon loose, finely ground or 2 bags English breakfast tea

3 teaspoons Lemon Powder (recipe follows) or grated lemon zest

1 tablespoon demerara sugar or coarse brown sugar

MUFFINS

1½ cups (204 grams) spelt flour

½ cup (70 grams) all-purpose flour

1 teaspoon kosher salt

½ cup granulated sugar

1½ tablespoon plus ½ tablespoon Arnold Palmer Powder

2 teaspoons baking powder

1 tablespoon poppy seeds

1 egg

1 cup buttermilk

8 tablespoons unsalted butter, melted and cooled

¼ cup plain whole milk yogurt

1 tablespoon lemon zest (2 small lemons)

¼ cup freshly squeezed lemon juice

MAKES 12 MUFFINS (OR 24 MINI MUFFINS)

TO MAKE THE LEMON POWDER: Peel long strips of zest from three medium lemons. Dry in a single layer in a dehydrator or on a baking sheet in a 170°F oven for two hours or until easily snapped. Cool and grind into powder in a spice grinder or mortar and pestle, yielding about 4 to 7 teaspoons. Use lemon powder in rice, sprinkled over broccoli, or stirred into hummus.

TO MAKE THE ARNOLD PALMER POWDER: Combine the ground tea, Lemon Powder or lemon zest, and demerara sugar in a small jar. Seal and shake spiritedly.

TO MAKE THE MUFFINS: Preheat the oven to 300°F. Lightly grease two 6-cup muffin pans. Whisk the flours, salt, granulated sugar, ½ tablespoon of the Arnold Palmer powder, baking powder, and poppy seeds for 30 seconds in a mixing bowl. In a separate bowl, whisk together the egg, buttermilk, butter, yogurt, lemon zest, and juice. Stir the liquid into the dry ingredients until combined. Do not overmix. Fill the muffin wells three-quarters full. Sprinkle a hearty pinch of the remaining Arnold Palmer powder on top. Bake until golden or when a toothpick comes out clean, 25 to 28 minutes.

SALLY'S MASALA CHAI PUMPKIN BREAD

Two things endeared me to Sally right away: her cheeky domino-playing chatter and her pumpkin bread. She has a big personality, and so does this bread. Be equally bold and customize your chai spices to taste. Note that this bread uses the Masala Chai Applesauce (page 9), so plan to make both.

MASALA CHAI POWDER

2 teaspoons ground cardamom

1½ teaspoons ground ginger

1 teaspoon ground cinnamon

¼ teaspoon finely ground black pepper

PUMPKIN BREAD

3½ cups (490 grams) all-purpose flour

3½ teaspoons baking powder

1½ cups sugar

4 teaspoons Masala Chai Powder

¾ teaspoon kosher salt

½ cup Masala Chai Applesauce (page 9)

¾ cup safflower, grapeseed, or other neutral oil

4 eggs

⅔ cup masala chai tea, brewed (1 bag or ½ tablespoon loose)

1 (15-ounce) can puréed pumpkin

1 cup chopped walnuts (optional)

MAKES 2 LARGE LOAVES (OR BAKE IN MINI LOAF PANS TO GIVE AS GIFTS)

TO MAKE THE MASALA CHAI POWDER: Mix the cardamom, ginger, cinnamon, and black pepper in a small jar. Seal it and shake spiritedly.

TO MAKE THE BREAD: Preheat the oven to 375°F. Grease two 9 by 5-inch loaf pans. In a large bowl, beat with a fork the flour, baking powder, sugar, Masala Chai Powder, and salt for 30 seconds. In a separate bowl, whisk the applesauce, oil, eggs, tea, and pumpkin. Stir the wet ingredients into the dry ingredients until just combined. Add the walnuts. Pour the batter into the prepared pans. Bake for 50 to 60 minutes or until a toothpick comes out clean. Cool for 10 minutes before slicing.

MASALA CHAI APPLESAUCE

Masala chai broth bronzes and infuses this fragrant applesauce. So many kinds of masala chai blends exist—use your favorite. I like Tazo's, which packs just enough sweetness with a hit of heat at the end. If you can't find Pink Lady apples, use four Fuji and two Granny Smith apples.

CHAI BROWN SUGAR

1 bag masala chai tea

¼ cup brown sugar

APPLESAUCE

6 Pink Lady apples, peeled, cored, and chopped

2 cups masala chai tea, brewed (4 bags or 2 tablespoons loose)

½ teaspoon fresh ginger, grated

1 tablespoon fresh lemon juice

⅛ teaspoon kosher salt

¼ cup Chai Brown Sugar

MAKES 3 CUPS

TO MAKE THE CHAI BROWN SUGAR: Combine the contents of one chai bag for every ¼ cup of brown sugar. Try Chai Brown Sugar in oatmeal or chocolate chip cookies.

TO MAKE THE APPLESAUCE: Over medium heat in an 8-quart stockpot, stir the apples, brewed chai, ginger, lemon juice, salt, and chai brown sugar until bubbling. Cover and lower the heat. Simmer and stir occasionally, until the liquid is cooked out, about 30 to 35 minutes. The applesauce will be chunky. If you prefer it smooth, purée with an immersion blender or in a blender.

CRANBERRY-COCONUT ROOIBOS OAT PORRIDGE

This is hot sustenance in a bowl on wickedly cold winter mornings. This recipe calls for steel-cut oats, which I prefer for their toothsome whole grain goodness. Some mornings you need all the help bran, endosperm, and germ can give. Swap out the coconut for orange zest if you like.

½ cup thick-cut unsweetened coconut flakes

3 cups water

1 cup steel-cut oats

2 bags rooibos

¼ teaspoon kosher salt

Maple syrup (optional)

¼ cup dried cranberries

MAKES 4 TO 6 SERVINGS

PREHEAT THE OVEN TO 300°F. Toast the coconut in a single layer on a sheet pan for 7 minutes, or until the flakes turn golden. Cool.

TO MAKE THE PORRIDGE: Bring the water to a boil in a 2-quart saucepan. Stir in the oats. Submerge the tisane bags with a wooden spoon, twirling the bag strings around the pot handle so they don't dangle. Turn the heat down. Cover the pot and simmer for 10 minutes or until most of the liquid has cooked out and the oats are your preferred texture. Press on the tisane bags to extract all the steeped liquid; discard the bags. Turn off the heat, stir in the salt, and sweeten to taste. Top with cranberries and coconut chips.

EARL GREY YOGURT PARFAITS

Fresh apricots must have their own secret handshake that involves a slap and a wink. Their short seasonal window may be why the fruit summons visions of dried, wrinkled discs for most people—a pity because a ripe apricot tinged with blush is something to savor. I prefer Mighty Leaf Earl Grey here for its juicy notes, which highlight the grapefruit. If apricot season has come and gone, swap in plums, peaches, or oranges.

EARL GREY YOGURT

2 cups plain whole milk yogurt

4 bags Earl Grey tea

PARFAITS

6 fresh ripe apricots, thinly sliced

1 large grapefruit, cut into segments
   with pith removed

MAKES 4 TO 6 PARFAITS

TO MAKE THE YOGURT: Pour the yogurt into a glass jar and submerge the tea bags (snip off the tags or hang them outside the jar). Seal the jar and refrigerate for up to four days, taking it out each day to jostle the contents and making sure the tea bags stay submerged. The longer the yogurt infuses, the stronger the tea taste will be. Before using, squeeze the tea bags over the jar to extract all the steeped liquid—you might be surprised how much comes out, and stir to mix. Earl Grey yogurt plays well with both chocolate and spice—dolloped on brownies or flourless chocolate cake and on gingerbread or pumpkin pie.

FOR EACH PARFAIT, LAYER IN ORDER: 1 tablespoon yogurt, half a sliced apricot, 1 tablespoon yogurt, two grapefruit slices, 1 tablespoon of yogurt, and finally another half sliced apricot.

MATCHA CHIA PUDDING PARFAITS

Chia seeds in liquid take on a gelatinous texture perfect for puddings, as in this parfait. Serve the parfaits in tall glasses to show off the layers.

MATCHA GREEN TEA CHIA PUDDING

1 teaspoon matcha green tea powder

1 cup whole milk

1 cup plain whole milk yogurt

6 teaspoons maple syrup

3 tablespoons chia seeds

PARFAITS

1 fresh ripe peach, puréed or mashed

¾ cup fresh raspberries, puréed or mashed

MAKES 4 SERVINGS

TO MAKE THE PUDDING: Place the matcha in a medium glass bowl. Heat the milk in a small saucepan over low heat to 175°F. Slowly pour in ¼ cup of the milk, whisking vigorously for 1 minute. When the matcha is completely dissolved, whisk in the remaining milk. Let cool 10 to 15 minutes. Whisk the yogurt into the matcha milk. Stir in the maple syrup and chia seeds. Chia seeds tend to clump so make sure they are all separately immersed. Cover and refrigerate 5 hours or overnight, until custardy.

TO ASSEMBLE: Layer in order 1 tablespoon peach, ½ cup chia pudding, 1 tablespoon raspberries.

BLUEBERRY BLACK TEA SMOOTHIE

Consider this bright purple smoothie for your morning caffeine fix. Prep the night before by preparing the beets, juice cubes, and tea. I use Fortnum & Mason English breakfast in this recipe, but you might prefer PG Tips for its robust astringency.

1 cup English breakfast tea, brewed and cooled (2 bags or 1 tablespoon loose)

1½ cups fresh blueberries

1 cup beets, peeled, cooked, and chopped (or precooked chopped)

½ banana

1½ teaspoons maple syrup

2 frozen cranberry juice cubes or ¼ cup cranberry juice

4 ice cubes

Pinch of kosher salt

MAKES 2 SERVINGS

Place ingredients in the blender as listed: tea, blueberries, beets, banana, maple syrup, cranberry ice cubes, ice, and salt. Blend until smooth. Add more ice if you prefer it frostier. Sweeten to taste.

GINGER-MANGO GREEN TEA SMOOTHIE

This one's not just for breakfast! This makes a great afternoon pick-me-up, thanks to the antioxidants in the green tea and spinach and the anti-inflammatory properties of the turmeric and vitamin C–rich mango.

1 cup jasmine green tea, brewed and cooled (1 bag or 1 teaspoon loose)

2¼ cups sliced fresh or frozen mango

2 cups firmly packed spinach

1 teaspoon ground ginger

¼ teaspoon turmeric powder

Pinch of kosher salt

2 teaspoons raw honey

2 ice cubes

MAKES 2 SERVINGS

Place ingredients in the blender as listed: tea, mango, spinach, ginger, turmeric powder, salt, honey, and ice. Blend until smooth. Add more ice cubes if you prefer it frostier. Sweeten to taste.

CHAMOMILE LASSI

Sip this floral, creamy chamomile lassi as a gentle wake-up first thing in the morning or as a soothing drink before bed. With just a hint of banana and maple syrup, this drink is only mildly sweet. I always use Choice Organic chamomile bags because the crushed petals incorporate more easily than full blossoms.

1 cup plain whole milk yogurt

½ cup whole milk

1 bag (cut open) chamomile

3 teaspoons maple syrup

1 banana, cut into 3 chunks

1 cup ice

Pinch of kosher salt

MAKES 2 TO 3 SERVINGS

Place ingredients in the blender as listed: yogurt, milk, crushed chamomile petals, maple syrup, banana, ice, and salt. Blend until smooth. Sweeten to taste.

PRESERVES

What sweeter reminder of summer on dark winter mornings than a dab of Sweet Tea Jelly or Strawberry Chamomile Jam on an English muffin? Stored in a dark, cool cabinet, these preserves should keep for up to nine months—meaning they will hold you until summer comes again. If you opt to skip the canning step, simply refrigerate the fresh preserves and enjoy them within two weeks. Otherwise, follow the canning directions below for all three recipes:

CANNING EQUIPMENT:

5-8 half-pint jelly jars with lids and bands (the exact number is specified in each recipe)

2 wire racks or metal trivets—1 sized for a pot large enough to hold all the jelly jars at once and 1 large enough to hold all the jelly jars on the counter

Large metal tongs shaped to grasp the jelly jars

Cooking thermometer

Large metal funnel

For the Buddha's Hand Marmalade, a cheesecloth and string

Put a saucer in the freezer. Rinse the jelly jar lids and bands in warm, soapy water. Fill a medium saucepan halfway with water and place it over low heat. Sterilize the lids and bands in the simmering water for 10 minutes. Put a canning rack or a barbecue trivet into a large heavy-bottomed stockpot, fill the stockpot three-quarters with water, and bring to a boil. Sterilize the jars in the boiling water for 15 minutes.

As the jars are sterilizing, follow the recipe for the preserve you are making, then return to step 3 below for the canning step.

Use tongs to move the jars from the pot onto a wire rack (keep the water boiling). Ladle the hot jelly, using a funnel, into each jar, leaving a 1/4-inch headspace. Remove any bubbles with a toothpick or wooden skewer. Wipe the jar rims clean with a damp paper towel. Secure the lid and band on each jar, turning until finger tight. Use tongs to move the jars. Place the jars into the large pot of boiling water. Process them for 10 minutes. Move them to the wire rack on the counter to cool. Listen for them to ping—the cheerful song that delights canners, the sign the lids have sealed. If a jar does not ping, store it in the refrigerator and use within two weeks.

SWEET TEA JELLY

I learned how to drink sweet tea in South Carolina as glasses of cool liquid courage for the sultry afternoons were passed around, condensation moistening our hands. This jelly is my best memory of back roads where peach trees were heavy with ripe fruit. At night in the small town, we would walk below the stars, telling each other stories to light our path. The idea with this jelly is to smear a bit on toast or shellac it on Mini Cherry Chai Cream Pies (page 92).

2 cups English breakfast tea
(⅓ cup loose)

2 tablespoons bottled lemon juice

1 package (1¾-ounce) powdered pectin

4 cups sugar

MAKES ABOUT 5 HALF-PINT JELLY JARS

Follow the canning preparation step 1 on page 18.

Pour the tea and lemon juice into a heavy-bottomed 2-quart saucepan set over medium-high heat. Stir in the pectin and bring to a boil. Stir in the sugar. Bring to a hard boil for 1 minute. Stir the jelly for 1 minute. Insert a thermometer into the pot, and once it has reached 220°F, turn off the heat to test the jelly.

Remove the plate from the freezer. Spoon a small amount of jelly onto the plate and put back in the freezer for 1 minute. Nudge into it with your finger. If it wrinkles, it's ready to can, following step 3 on page 18. If not, cook it for a bit longer and test it again. Alternately, let it cool completely and store in glass jars in the refrigerator for two weeks.

Buddha's Hand Rooibos
Marmalade (page 22)

Sweet Tea Jelly
(page 19)

Strawberry
Chamomile Jam
(opposite)

STRAWBERRY CHAMOMILE JAM

If you have never made jam but always hankered to, start here: Strawberry jam is easy!

2 pounds fresh ripe strawberries, washed, dried, stemmed, and sliced (6 cups)

6 cups sugar, divided

3 bags (cut open) chamomile

2 tablespoons freshly squeezed lemon juice (1 medium lemon)

1 package (1¾-ounce) powdered pectin

MAKES ABOUT 6 HALF-PINT JARS

Stir the sliced strawberries, 2 cups of the sugar, and the crushed chamomile petals to coat in a large bowl. Cover and refrigerate overnight or for 8 hours.

Follow the canning preparation step 1 on page 18.

Pour half the strawberries and their juices into an 8-quart heavy-bottomed stockpot and crush them with a potato masher. Add the other berries, the liquid, and any undissolved sugar from the bowl into the pot. Stir in the lemon juice and pectin.

Bring the pot of jam to a full rolling boil while continuously stirring. You'll notice the jam will change colors and look foamy. Once stirring does not calm the bubbles, boil the jam hard for 1 minute.

Stir in the remaining 4 cups of sugar, aiming for another full rolling boil that can't be stirred down. Boil hard for 1 minute and keep stirring. Once the temperature gets to 220°F, turn off the heat to test the jam.

Remove the plate from the freezer. Spoon a small amount of jam onto the plate, and put it back in the freezer for 1 minute. Nudge into it with your finger. If it wrinkles, it's ready to can, following step 3 on page 18. If not, cook it for a bit longer and test it again. Turn off the heat and quickly skim any foam. Alternately, let it cool completely and store in glass jars in the refrigerator for two weeks.

BUDDHA'S HAND ROOIBOS MARMALADE

When winter descends in California, I begin to scout for the yellow tentacles of the pungent lemon-grass-perfumed Buddha's hand. Begin plotting your Buddha's hand reconnaissance mission now.

1 Buddha's hand

10 Meyer lemons

5½ cups sugar, divided

6 cups rooibos tea, brewed
(4 bags or 2 tablespoons loose,
steeped 10 minutes)

MAKES 7 TO 8 HALF-PINT JARS

TO PREPARE THE CITRUSES: Cut the Buddha's hand in half and into fingers. Peel off the zest. Mince the zest into confetti and place into a large non-reactive bowl. Reserve the pith in a separate bowl. Quarter the lemons. Cut out and reserve the lemon membranes and seeds with the Buddha's hand pith. Slice the lemon quarters into ¼-inch strips. Toss them in with the zest. Stir in 2 cups of the sugar to coat the zest and lemon. Secure the pith, lemon seeds and membranes in cheesecloth with string, making a pouch. Burrow the pith pouch into the zest and lemon. Cover and refrigerate for 48 hours.

Follow canning preparation step 1 on page 18.

Toss the prepared citruses, the remaining 3½ cups of sugar, and the pith pouch into a large heavy-bottomed stockpot. Pour in the rooibos and bring to a boil, stirring regularly. Keep the marmalade at a vigorous temperature and stir frequently.

Once the marmalade reaches 220°F, which can take anywhere from 30 to 90 minutes, test its viscosity. Remove the plate from the freezer. Spoon a small amount of marmalade onto the plate, and put it back in the freezer for 1 minute. Nudge into it with your finger. If it wrinkles, it's ready to can, following step 3 on page 18. If not, cook it for a bit longer and test it again. Alternately, let it cool completely and store in glass jars in the refrigerator for two weeks.

MIDDAY TEA

BRUNCH

Oat Pancakes with Chamomile-Scented Strawberries,
Spiked Crème Fraîche, and Lemon Curd

Butternut Squash Hash with Fried Eggs and Lemony Kale Slaw

Green Tea Egg Wraps Stuffed with Artichoke Cream and Squash

Summer Squash Gruyère Quiche

SALADS

Rainbow Salad with Smoky Chickpeas

Spinach Salad with Pears and Masala Chai Maple Pecans

California Tea Leaf Salad

Earl Grey Soba Noodle Salad

Teabbouleh

DRINKS

Earl Grey Whey Soda

Peach Tea Shrub

PROVISION

Green Tea Vinegar

The cicada's dry monotony breaks
over me. The days are bright
and free, bright and free.
—JANE KENYON

The middle of the day brings a welcome break.
Whatever worries the morning ushered in can
be set aside for a spell as we rest and refuel.
Often it is at lunch that tea comes poured over
ice, cubes cracking and glass glistening with
condensation. Nudge open a book, listen to
music, meet up with a friend. It is not too late
to change course. Midday is your time to chart
the rest of your day.

OAT PANCAKES *with* CHAMOMILE-SCENTED STRAWBERRIES, SPIKED CRÈME FRAÎCHE, *and* LEMON CURD

This recipe may have more moving parts than you are used to slinging for breakfast, but it would be excellent to celebrate Mother's Day or a birthday. The chamomile sugar, strawberries, crème fraîche, and lemon curd can all be made ahead of time, and of course the pancakes are plenty delicious with only one or two of the toppings. The leftover egg whites from the lemon curd are perfect for the Jasmine Cacao Nib Meringues (page 95).

MAKES 8 TO 10 PANCAKES

CHAMOMILE SUGAR AND CHAMOMILE-SCENTED STRAWBERRIES

½ cup sugar

2 bags (cut open) chamomile

1 pound organic strawberries, rinsed, patted dry, hulled, and quartered (2 cups)

SPIKED CRÈME FRAÎCHE

1 tablespoon brown sugar

1 tablespoon bourbon

1 (7½-ounce) container crème fraîche

LEMON CURD

4 large egg yolks

½ cup sugar

⅓ cup freshly squeezed lemon juice (about 3 small lemons)

1 tablespoon plus 1 teaspoon lemon zest (about 2 small lemons)

4 tablespoons unsalted butter, room temperature

OAT PANCAKES

1 cup oat flour or rolled oats finely ground in a food processor

1 cup all-purpose flour

1 teaspoon kosher salt

3 tablespoons Chamomile Sugar (recipe follows)

1 teaspoon baking powder

½ teaspoon baking soda

1½ cups buttermilk

2 eggs, separated

½ tablespoon unsalted butter

(CONTINUED)

OAT PANCAKES *with* CHAMOMILE-SCENTED STRAWBERRIES, SPIKED CRÈME FRAÎCHE, *and* LEMON CURD

(CONTINUED)

TO MAKE THE CHAMOMILE SUGAR: Shake together the sugar and crushed chamomile petals in a sealed glass jar. Rest the sugar at least 5 minutes or longer.

TO MAKE THE CHAMOMILE-SCENTED STRAWBERRIES: Stir the strawberries in a bowl with 3 tablespoons of chamomile sugar to coat. Cover and chill 30 minutes.

TO MAKE THE SPIKED CRÈME FRAÎCHE: Whisk the brown sugar and bourbon into the crème fraîche in a small bowl. Cover and chill 30 minutes or longer.

TO MAKE THE LEMON CURD: Bring a 2-quart saucepan or the bottom of a double boiler filled halfway with water to a simmer. In the smaller pot or the top of the double boiler resting over the simmering water, whisk together the yolks and sugar. Add the lemon juice and zest. Whisk for several minutes until the curd becomes glossy and thickens. Remove from heat and stir in the butter. Spoon the curd into a glass jar. Cool to room temperature before refrigerating.

TO MAKE THE PANCAKES: Whisk together the flours, salt, chamomile sugar, baking powder, and baking soda in a big bowl. In a separate bowl, whisk the buttermilk into the egg yolks. With a clean whisk, beat the egg whites in another small bowl until frothy. Mix the wet ingredients into the dry ingredients until just combined. Fold in the egg whites. Heat a medium skillet on medium-low heat until a drop of water sizzles, and let a small knob of butter melt in the pan. Ladle about ¼ cup batter at a time, cooking the pancakes about 3 minutes on the first side and about 2 minutes on the flip side. Serve topped with the strawberries, crème fraîche, and lemon curd.

BUTTERNUT SQUASH HASH *with* FRIED EGGS *and* LEMONY KALE SLAW

This is a brunch served to guests I especially esteem, better known as other people who may not rise and shine quite so early. Feel free to use a 12-ounce bag of precut butternut squash and bagged baby kale to save time.

MAKES 2 TO 3 SERVINGS

SMOKY SPICE

½ teaspoon red pepper flakes

½ teaspoon loose, finely ground lapsang souchong tea

¼ teaspoon smoked paprika

¼ teaspoon ground cumin

LEMONY KALE SLAW

1 head of kale, ribs torn out, leaves shredded

4 to 5 Brussels sprouts, shredded (1 cup)

1 tablespoon freshly squeezed lemon juice (1 small lemon)

1 tablespoon olive oil

¼ teaspoon kosher salt

1 clove garlic, minced

BUTTERNUT SQUASH HASH

1 pound 4 ounces butternut squash, peeled, seeded and medium chopped (3 cups)

2 tablespoons olive oil

1 medium yellow onion, chopped (1 cup)

¼ green bell pepper, chopped (⅓ cup)

1 teaspoon kosher salt

½ teaspoon Smoky Spice

4 eggs

TO MAKE THE SMOKY SPICE: Stir together the red pepper, tea, paprika, and cumin. Use leftover smoky spice in Smoky Roasted Chickpeas (page 34).

TO MAKE THE SLAW: Massage the lemon juice, olive oil, and salt into the kale and Brussels sprouts shreds until they are glossy and compressed. Add the garlic and toss.

TO MAKE THE HASH: Bring a 2-quart saucepan filled halfway with water to a gentle boil. Cook the squash until fork-tender but not mushy, about 7 minutes. Drain and cool for 5 minutes and pat dry. Place a 12-inch fry pan over medium heat for 1 minute. Drizzle in the oil to coat. Sauté the onion and bell pepper until the onion is almost translucent, about 5 minutes. Add the squash and cook for 12 minutes, stirring occasionally, or until the edges have browned and crisped. Finish with the salt and smoky spice.

TO SERVE: In another skillet, fry the eggs to your liking. Serve atop the hash and alongside the slaw.

GREEN TEA EGG WRAPS STUFFED *with* ARTICHOKE CREAM *and* SQUASH

I do like Green Tea Egg Wraps, and you will, too. These crêpes are one part Dr. Seuss and one part Shen Nung, the result of a happy Monday morning accident, served here with our favorite Sunday morning filling. Leftover artichoke cream makes an easy sauce for pasta. (Thin the cream with a little pasta water.)

MAKES 2 TO 4 SERVINGS

ARTICHOKE CREAM

5 artichoke hearts from 1 (14-ounce) can plus 2 tablespoons soaking liquid

1 cup whole milk ricotta

½ teaspoon kosher salt

⅛ teaspoon freshly ground black pepper

SAUTÉED SQUASH

1 tablespoon olive oil

1 medium leek, white part only cut in half, washed, and sliced (1 cup)

1 medium zucchini, julienned (2 cups)

2 medium yellow squash, julienned (2 cups)

¼ teaspoon kosher salt

Pinch of freshly ground black pepper

¼ cup vegetable stock or Green Tea Stock (page 86)

GREEN TEA WRAPS

1 teaspoon matcha green tea powder

4 tablespoons half-and-half

2 tablespoons all-purpose flour

4 eggs

¼ teaspoon kosher salt

Pinch of freshly ground black pepper

4 teaspoons pine nuts

TO MAKE THE ARTICHOKE CREAM: Purée the artichoke hearts, artichoke-heart soaking liquid, ricotta, salt, and pepper in a blender or food processor until smooth.

TO MAKE THE SQUASH: Heat a 12-inch fry pan over medium-low heat for 1 minute. Drizzle in the oil to coat. Cook the leeks for 3 minutes. Add the squash, salt, and pepper and cook for 2 minutes. Pour in the stock. Cover and cook for 5 minutes, or until the vegetables are fork-tender. Turn off the heat.

TO MAKE THE WRAPS: Spoon the matcha into a medium bowl. Pour the half-and-half into a saucepan set over low heat. When bubbles break out on the surface, turn off the heat. Whisk the half-and-half into the matcha vigorously for 1 minute, or until clump-free. Whisk in the flour until clump-free. Whisk in one egg at a time, and add the salt and pepper. Place an 8½-inch nonstick skillet over medium-low heat for 2 minutes until a drop of water sizzles. Make one wrap at a time, ladling in ¼ cup batter and swirling the skillet to coat. Cook for 2 minutes, or until the surface bubbles. Flip and cook for 1 minute more. Continue with the remaining batter. To serve: Down the center of each wrap layer artichoke cream, sautéed squash, and a sprinkle of pine nuts. Roll and eat immediately.

SUMMER SQUASH GRUYÈRE QUICHE

The rustic quality of spelt really shines in this flaky crust, which is flavored with mint, as is the cheesy vegetable filling. I recommend Choice Organic Teas' Moroccan Mint.

SPELT PIE CRUST

¾ cup (102 grams) spelt flour

½ cup (70 grams) all-purpose flour

½ teaspoon kosher salt

8 tablespoons unsalted butter, cold and cubed

5 to 6 tablespoons Moroccan mint green tea, brewed and cooled

QUICHE

1 tablespoon olive oil

1 small zucchini, cubed

1 medium yellow summer squash, cubed

1 shallot, sliced

¾ cup heavy cream

3 eggs

¼ teaspoon fennel seeds

½ teaspoon from 1 bag (cut open) or from loose Moroccan mint green tea, finely ground

¼ teaspoon kosher salt

3½ ounces Gruyère cheese or Jarlsberg cheese, cubed (½ cup)

MAKES 6 TO 8 SERVINGS

TO MAKE THE CRUST: Mix the flours and salt in a large bowl. Using your fingers, rub the butter cubes into the flour until combined and pea-sized. Mix the cold tea into the flour with your hands until the dough coheres. Form the dough into a ball and wrap in plastic wrap; refrigerate for 30 minutes or until firm as a baseball. Lightly flour a work surface, your hands, and a rolling pin. Roll away from the middle of the dough and rotate the dough. Roll and rotate until the dough is ⅛ inch thick. Fit the dough into a 10-inch tart or pie pan. Trim the excess above the pan sides but keep the crust walls tall. Refrigerate 30 minutes.

PREHEAT THE OVEN TO 425°F. Fit a sheet of aluminum foil into the crust and pour in pie weights, uncooked rice, or dried beans. Bake 20 minutes. Remove the weights and foil and bake the crust 3 to 5 minutes longer. Lower the oven to 400°F.

Meanwhile, place a 12-inch fry pan over medium-low heat for 1 minute. Swirl the oil into the pan. Sauté the zucchini, squash, and shallot for 5 minutes. Turn off the heat and cool. Whisk the cream and eggs in a bowl. Stir in the fennel, tea, salt, Gruyère, and squash. Pour into the cooled crust.

Bake for 20 to 25 minutes or until a toothpick comes out clean. Cool 10 to 15 minutes before slicing.

RAINBOW SALAD *with* SMOKY CHICKPEAS

Almost all of the swatches on a color wheel are represented in this salad. The roasted chickpeas use the same Smoky Spice as the Butternut Squash Hash (page 28) and can make a protein-packed snack.

SMOKY CHICKPEAS

1 (15½-ounce) can chickpeas, drained and rinsed

2 teaspoons safflower, grapeseed, or other neutral oil

1 teaspoon Smoky Spice (page 28)

⅛ teaspoon kosher salt

RED PEPPER VINAIGRETTE

½ roasted red bell pepper, peeled, seeded, cored, and coarsely chopped (½ cup)

2 tablespoons distilled white vinegar

1 teaspoon tomato paste

1 small clove garlic, coarsely chopped

½ teaspoon kosher salt

Freshly ground black pepper

⅓ cup olive oil

SALAD

2 cups organic corn kernels, steamed and cooled

1½ cups shredded purple cabbage

¼ cup basil leaves, shredded

8 mini fresh mozzarella balls, quartered

MAKES 3 TO 4 SERVINGS

TO MAKE THE CHICKPEAS: Preheat the oven to 400°F. Line an 18-inch sheet pan with parchment paper. Remove the chickpea skins by pinching the round end; the skins should slip off. Rub the chickpeas with a paper towel to dry. Toss them in a bowl with the oil, Smoky Spice, and salt and tumble them onto the sheet pan in a single layer. Roast for 30 minutes.

TO MAKE THE VINAIGRETTE: Purée the bell pepper, vinegar, tomato paste, garlic, salt, and pepper in a blender until smooth, drizzling in olive oil until the dressing comes together.

TO ASSEMBLE THE SALAD: Toss the ingredients with ⅓ cup vinaigrette.

SPINACH SALAD *with* PEARS *and* MASALA CHAI MAPLE PECANS

The holidays deserve a festive salad, so plan ahead for this one. The only part of this recipe that takes time is the Masala Chai Maple Syrup, which gets better the longer it steeps. Consider it time well spent.

MASALA CHAI MAPLE SYRUP

2 cups maple syrup

2 tablespoons loose masala chai tea

MASALA CHAI MAPLE PECANS

¼ cup Masala Chai Maple Syrup

⅛ teaspoon kosher salt

1 cup pecans, divided

MAPLE MUSTARD VINAIGRETTE

2 teaspoons Dijon mustard

2 teaspoons raw apple cider vinegar

2 teaspoons Masala Chai Maple Syrup

1 small clove garlic, minced

Kosher salt and freshly ground black
   pepper

2 tablespoons olive oil

SALAD

8 cups (5 ounces) firmly packed baby
   spinach

1 pear, chopped (1 cup), divided

MAKES 4 SERVINGS

TO MAKE THE MASALA CHAI MAPLE SYRUP: Measure the chai into a quart glass jar. Pour in the syrup. Seal and jostle the jar to suspend the tea. Refrigerate. Two weeks to one month later, strain out the leaves, pressing on them over the jar to extract every sweet steeped drop. Refrigerate and use the syrup by the date on the original bottle. The syrup also tastes dreamy with oatmeal, waffles, or plain yogurt.

TO MAKE THE PECANS: Preheat the oven to 350°F. Line a sheet pan with parchment paper. Stir the syrup, salt, and pecans in a medium bowl to coat. Arrange on the pan in a single layer. Bake 15 minutes, rotating the pan halfway through. Cool.

TO MAKE THE VINAIGRETTE: Stir the mustard, vinegar, maple syrup, garlic, and salt and pepper to taste. Whisk in the oil until combined.

TO ASSEMBLE THE SALAD: Toss together the spinach, a ½ cup of the pears, and a ½ cup of the pecans. Dress right before serving. Season with salt and pepper. Scatter the remaining pecans and pears onto each portion, as they tend to fall to the bottom.

CALIFORNIA TEA LEAF SALAD

The Burmese tea leaf salads served in the two very popular Burmese restaurants down the street from my apartment in San Francisco inspired this California version, which subs in our local fruits, nuts, and vegetables. Fermented tea leaves are the by-product of the Green Tea Vinegar (page 42), so head there first. The Fried Split Peas and Garlic Chips make delicious garnishes for any salad!

FRIED SPLIT PEAS

½ cup split peas

3 tablespoons safflower, grapeseed, or other neutral oil

¼ teaspoon kosher salt

GARLIC CHIPS

¼ cup safflower, grapeseed, or other neutral oil

1 head of garlic, peeled and sliced into ¼-inch slivered coins

SALAD

2 heads romaine lettuce, shredded

2 avocados, pitted and diced

3 tablespoons sesame seeds

6 tablespoons seeded, minced jalapeño

¼ cup plus 2 tablespoons raw unsalted sunflower seeds

¾ cup firm tomatoes, diced

2 tablespoons Fermented Green Tea Leaves (page 42)

1 lemon, quartered

MAKES 4 TO 6 SERVINGS

TO MAKE THE PEAS: Soak the split peas for 8 hours or overnight on the counter, covered by 1 to 2 inches of water. Drain and dry well. Line two large plates with paper towels and place them on the counter near the stovetop. Place a 12-inch fry pan over medium heat for 1 minute. Swirl the oil into the pan to coat. Fry the peas, stirring constantly for 8 to 10 minutes, or until they shrink, begin to wrinkle, and dull in color. Transfer with a slotted spoon onto a lined plate to drain. Salt when cool.

TO MAKE THE GARLIC CHIPS: Place a 12-inch fry pan over medium-low heat for 1 minute. Swirl the oil into the pan to coat. Fry the garlic, stirring occasionally, until golden, about 3 minutes. Transfer with a slotted spoon into a fine-mesh sieve placed over a small bowl. Reserve all the garlic-infused oil from the bowl and the pan to dress the salad. Transfer the garlic chips to the other lined plate.

TO ASSEMBLE THE SALAD: Toss the lettuce in a large shallow bowl. Part of the allure of this salad is the assemblage, so mound the avocado, sesame seeds, jalapeño, sunflower seeds, tomatoes, fried peas, and garlic chips to display the ingredients before the final toss, with the fermented tea leaves in the middle. Dress with the garlic-infused oil, freshly squeezed lemon juice, and salt and pepper to taste. Toss and serve.

EARL GREY SOBA NOODLE SALAD

Earl Grey introduces its citrusy tannins to crispy cabbage, sweet red bell pepper, raw carrot ribbons, and caramelized onions for a refreshing chilled salad, perfect for picnics. If you can stand to wait, this salad tastes even better the next day.

MAKES 6 TO 8 SERVINGS

EARL GREY DRESSING

⅓ cup Earl Grey tea, brewed and cooled

½ teaspoon toasted sesame oil

2½ teaspoons maple syrup

¾ teaspoon kosher salt

3 teaspoons distilled white vinegar

2 small cloves garlic, minced

1½ teaspoon fresh ginger, minced

2 teaspoons grapeseed, safflower, or other neutral oil

1 teaspoon Sriracha

SOBA NOODLE SALAD

1 teaspoon safflower, grapeseed, or other neutral flavored oil

1 small red onion, thinly sliced (¾ cup)

2 carrots, grated into ribbons (2 cups)

½ red bell pepper, seeded and sliced into matchsticks

¼ head purple cabbage, thinly sliced and separated into ribbons (2 cups)

3 oranges, cut into segments with pith removed (1½ cups)

½ bunch fresh curly parsley leaves, finely chopped (½ cup)

1 tablespoon sesame seeds

8 ounces soba noodles

TO MAKE THE DRESSING: Whisk together the tea, sesame oil, maple syrup, salt, vinegar, garlic, ginger, oil, and Sriracha.

Drizzle the oil into a medium pan, set over low heat, swirling to coat. Sauté the onion until caramelized, 10 minutes. Toss the onion, carrot, bell pepper, cabbage, oranges, parsley, and sesame seeds in a large bowl. Put a 2-quart saucepan two-thirds full of water over medium heat. When boiling, add the noodles and cook according to the package instructions. Drain and run them under cold water to cool. Add the noodles to the salad. Dress and toss to coat.

TEABBOULEH

A few splashes of Green Tea Vinegar (page 42) transforms tabbouleh to teabbouleh. Serve a vibrant bowl as the centerpiece of midday meze, with White Bean Walnut Spread (page 52), Tea Crackers (page 55), and Creamy Cucumber Roll-Ups (page 47). Swap out the bulgur for quinoa or millet to make it wheat-free. This tastes even better if you let the ingredients marinate, so make it ahead if you can.

1 cup coarsely ground bulgur

2 cups water

1 medium tomato, chopped (1 cup)

1 bunch curly parsley leaves, finely
   chopped (4 cups)

2½ tablespoons chopped scallions
   (green parts only)

1 teaspoon kosher salt

⅛ teaspoon freshly ground black pepper

6 tablespoons Green Tea Vinegar
   (page 42)

1 tablespoon olive oil

MAKES 4 TO 6 SERVINGS

Bring the bulgur and water to boil in a 2-quart saucepan. Cover and lower the heat to simmer for 12 minutes. Turn off the heat and keep covered 5 minutes. Drain the bulgur in a fine-mesh sieve and rinse with cold water to cool. In a large bowl, toss the bulgur, tomato, parsley, scallions, salt, pepper, vinegar, and olive oil. Cover and refrigerate until chilled.

EARL GREY WHEY SODA

This fizzy drink is reminiscent of orange creamsicles. If you make your own labneh, you can use the whey by-product here, or substitute buttermilk. Make it a Long Beach cocktail by adding 2 parts of Earl Grey Whey Soda to 1 part good gin.

EARL GREY SIMPLE SYRUP

½ cup water

½ cup sugar

1 tablespoon loose or 2 bags Earl Grey tea

WHEY SODA

½ cup whey or buttermilk

750 ml sparkling water

2 cups ice

MAKES 4 SERVINGS

TO MAKE THE SIMPLE SYRUP: Place the water, sugar, and tea in a 2-quart saucepan set over high heat. Stir occasionally for 3 minutes, or until the liquid becomes clear and the sugar has dissolved. Turn off the heat. Steep 10 minutes more. Strain through a fine-mesh sieve if using loose. Press on the leaves or bags to extract all the steeped liquid; discard the leaves or bags. Cool for 45 minutes.

TO MAKE THE SODA: Mix together the simple syrup, whey or buttermilk, and sparkling water in a pitcher. Pour ½ cup soda over ½ cup ice per serving.

PEACH TEA SHRUB

Peach tea gets an old-fashioned makeover in this versatile, sour-sweet shrub. A little goes a long way in salad dressings and creative cocktails. With sparkling water it makes a fun, effervescent riff on iced tea.

3 medium fresh, ripe peaches, rinsed, pitted, and chopped (4½ cups)

1 tablespoon loose English breakfast tea, finely ground

1 cup sugar

1 cup champagne vinegar

MAKES 12 SERVINGS

Place the peaches in a large nonreactive bowl. Pour the finely ground tea and sugar over them. Stir to coat. Cover and refrigerate 8 hours or overnight. Spoon the peaches, including all the sugar and tea bits, into a large quart-sized glass jar. Muddle the peaches in the jar and pour the vinegar over. Seal and refrigerate for about two weeks. Taste a spoonful at the end of the first week. The flavor should be tart. By the second week it will have mellowed quite a bit to just a slight tang. Strain through a fine-mesh sieve set over a non-reactive bowl, pressing on the peaches to extract all the steeped liquid. Discard the pulp. Pour the strained shrub into a clean pint-size glass jar. Store refrigerated for up to two months.

GREEN TEA VINEGAR

This is simple and sublime. At two weeks, its taste is reminiscent of green tea. By week four, it is completely infused with the tea's mellow tannins and nutty green essence. Don't discard the fermented tea leaves, as they are the star in the California Tea Leaf Salad (page 36). Store the vinegar in a long-necked bottle away from heat and light, and use it for Teabbouleh (page 39) or in any salad dressing.

¼ cup loose Dragon Well green tea

4 cups distilled white vinegar

MAKES 4 CUPS (32 OUNCES)

Place the tea leaves in a large glass jar. Heat the vinegar over low heat to 175°F. Pour the warm vinegar over the tea in a swirling motion, ensuring at least a ½-inch headspace from the top. Seal the jar and store in a cool, dark area for two weeks to one month. Strain through a fine-mesh sieve. Press on the leaves to extract all the steeped liquid. Transfer to a clean jar and store in a cool, dark place. Reserve the tea leaves to use right away.

AFTERNOON TEA

BITES

Berta's Egg Salad Sandwiches

Fresh Fennel Lychee Spring Rolls with Black Tea Dipping Sauce

Creamy Cucumber Roll-ups

Green Tea Guacamole with Grapefruit Tea Toast

Lapsang Honey–Drizzled Fig, Arugula, and Parmesan Tea Toast

French Lentil, Carrot Curl, and Moroccan Mint Sauce Tea Toast

White Bean Walnut Spread with Roasted Tomato Tea Toast

NIBBLES

Hurricane Popcorn with Tea Furikake

Tea Crackers with Herbed Labneh

DRINKS

New Orleans Iced Tea

Watermelon Tea Fresca

Forbidden Chai Horchata

Meeting together over afternoon tea is a treat.
While brunch has its ardent fans, afternoon tea,
with its nibbles and bites, its teapots passed from cup
to cup, is something truly special. Sip the sunshine
while the afternoon is still upon us.

Meanwhile, let us have a sip of tea.
The afternoon glow is brightening the bamboos,
the fountains are bubbling with delight,
the soughing of the pines is heard in our kettle.
Let us dream of evanescence, and
linger in the beautiful foolishness of things.
—OKAKURA KAKUZŌ

BERTA'S EGG SALAD SANDWICHES

My Tía Berta makes my favorite egg salad, which owes its fine texture to grated eggs. I swap out her dill and relish for fresh thyme and tea mayonnaise, but we both agree that challah makes egg salad extra special.

MAKES 4 TO 6 SANDWICHES

LAPSANG SOUCHONG MAYONNAISE

1 egg yolk

1 teaspoon distilled white vinegar

¼ teaspoon loose lapsang souchong tea, finely ground

¼ teaspoon Lapsang Souchong Salt (page 52)

¼ teaspoon mustard powder

½ cup olive oil

Pinch of freshly ground black pepper

1 teaspoon freshly squeezed lemon juice

EGG SALAD

6 hard-boiled eggs

2 tablespoons minced white onion

½ teaspoon fresh thyme leaves, coarsely chopped

⅓ cup Lapsang Souchong Mayonnaise

1 teaspoon yellow mustard

Pinch of black pepper

⅛ teaspoon Lapsang Souchong Salt (page 52)

¾ teaspoon freshly squeezed lemon juice

1½ cups arugula leaves

8 to 12 slices challah bread (or your favorite)

TO MAKE THE MAYONNAISE: Whisk the yolk, vinegar, lapsang souchong powder, salt, and mustard powder together. Add the oil in a thin steady stream, constantly whisking until the mayonnaise is creamy and thoroughly combined. Whisk in the pepper and lemon juice.

TO MAKE THE EGG SALAD: Grate the eggs into a bowl. Stir in the onion, thyme, mayonnaise, mustard, pepper, salt, and lemon juice until well-blended. Portion ½ cup arugula and ¼ cup egg salad per sandwich, or to taste.

FRESH FENNEL LYCHEE SPRING ROLLS
with BLACK TEA DIPPING SAUCE

My friend Pam taught me how to make spring rolls and I became hooked. Roll them like little burritos. If fresh lychees are out of season, use canned lychees or mandarin oranges—just rinse and dry before using. Sambal oelek is an Indonesian chili paste available in Asian groceries or online, but Sriracha is fine, too.

SPRING ROLLS

3½ ounces thin rice noodles (also called maifun or rice sticks)

½ fennel bulb, cored and cut into matchsticks

20 fresh lychees, peeled and chunked

½ cup loosely packed fresh mint leaves

3 green onions, chopped (greens only)

20 (22 centimeter size) rice paper wrappers

TEA DIPPING SAUCE

2 tablespoons (or more to taste) English breakfast tea, brewed and strong

¼ cup rice vinegar

1 clove garlic, minced

1½ tablespoons raw honey

1 teaspoon sambal oelek or Sriracha

MAKES 20 SPRING ROLLS (SERVES 6 TO 8)

TO MAKE THE SPRING ROLLS: Bring 4 quarts of water to a boil in a 2-quart saucepan. Turn the heat off and soak the rice noodles for 10 minutes. Drain and rinse under cold water until cool.

Fill a pie pan (or any large shallow pan) with warm water. Position a cutting board next to the pan. Place each ingredient in its own bowl at the top of the board in this order: wrappers, fennel, noodles, lychee, mint leaves, onions. Now you're ready to roll.

Submerge a wrapper in the warm water until soft and pliable, between 10 to 15 seconds. Place it on the board and layer fennel sticks, a pinch of noodles, four lychee quarters, several mint leaves, and a sprinkle of onion. Fold the top over the filling. Bring the bottom up, pulling gently but snugly. Seal the sides tightly toward the center. Serve with dipping sauce.

TO MAKE THE DIPPING SAUCE: Whisk the vinegar, garlic, honey, sambal oelek, and tea in a small bowl. Add more tea to taste, if desired.

CREAMY CUCUMBER ROLL-UPS

These roll-ups refresh the classic afternoon tea sandwich of cream cheese and cucumber with Middle Eastern flair. Serve with iced Moroccan mint tea and dishes of olives, crudités, and hummus.

4 sheets lavash or other thin, flexible flatbread

1 cup Herbed Labneh (page 55)

1 medium cucumber, peeled and sliced in thin rounds

MAKES 16 ROLL-UPS (SERVES 4 TO 6)

Spread ¼ cup Herbed Labneh on each lavash. Tile the cucumber from top to bottom until the lavash is covered. Roll the lavash and seal. Lay it seam-side down. Cut in half and half again, so each lavash makes four roll-ups. Serve immediately.

GREEN TEA GUACAMOLE *with* GRAPEFRUIT TEA TOAST

In this scintillating version of avocado toast, guacamole is elevated by matcha green tea and garnished with grapefruit. These toasts and Watermelon Tea Frescas (page 59) make a fiesta.

GREEN TEA GUACAMOLE

1 teaspoon olive oil

6 tablespoons diced white onion

⅛ teaspoon balsamic vinegar

2 avocados, pitted and chopped

3 kumquats, seeded and minced

2 small or 1 large clove garlic, minced

1 teaspoon matcha green tea powder

½ teaspoon Sriracha

1 teaspoon kosher salt

¾ teaspoon freshly squeezed lime juice (¼ lime)

TEA TOAST

10 to 12 slices sourdough bread, toasted

1 large or 2 medium grapefruit, peeled and cut into segments (10 to 12 supremes)

1 breakfast radish, thinly sliced (10 to 12 rounds)

MAKES 10 TO 12 TOASTS

TO MAKE THE GUACAMOLE: Place a 2-quart fry pan over medium-low heat for 1 minute. Swirl in the oil to coat. Stir in the onion. Turn the heat down to low. Sauté the onions for 15 minutes, stirring occasionally. Drizzle in the vinegar and turn off the heat. Cool for 5 minutes. Smash the avocado in a medium bowl until desired consistency. Stir in the onion, kumquats, garlic, matcha, Sriracha, salt, and lime juice.

TO ASSEMBLE: Heartily smear each toast with guacamole. Top with a grapefruit segment and round of radish.

Clockwise from the top:

French Lentil, Carrot Curl, and Moroccan Mint Sauce Tea Toast, (page 51)

White Bean Walnut Spread with Roasted Tomato Tea Toast, (page 52)

Lapsang Honey-Drizzled Fig, Arugula, and Parmesan Tea Toast, (page 50)

Green Tea Guacamole with Grapefruit Tea Toast

LAPSANG HONEY–DRIZZLED FIG, ARUGULA, *and* PARMESAN TEA TOAST

To me, fresh figs are one of life's true delicacies. I even dedicated a poem to them, "Ode to a Black Mission." Here the plump perfection of figs meet peppery arugula, slightly sour levain, and salty Parmigiano-Reggiano, gilded by subtly smoked honey.

LAPSANG HONEY

1 cup raw honey

3 tablespoons loose lapsang souchong tea

TEA TOAST

1½ cups arugula

5 ounces Parmigiano-Reggiano, thinly sliced (18 slices)

6 large ripe figs, quartered

6 tablespoons Lapsang Honey

6 slices seedy wheat levain bread, sliced and toasted

MAKES 6 TOASTS

TO MAKE THE HONEY: Pour the honey over the tea leaves in a glass jar. Seal and store in a dark, cool place for twelve days. Strain the tea-infused honey through a fine-mesh sieve into a clean glass jar. You can steep the leftover tea leaves in 2 cups boiling water for pre-sweetened tea.

TO ASSEMBLE: On each toast layer arugula, three slices Parmigiano-Reggiano, four fig quarters, and a drizzle of honey.

FRENCH LENTIL, CARROT CURL, *and* MOROCCAN MINT SAUCE TEA TOAST

Moroccan mint green tea accents this Mediterranean-inspired toast. Try the reduction sauce over steamed cauliflower or mashed parsnip and potatoes.

1 cup French du Puy lentils

3 cups water

1 bag lapsang souchong tea

1 tablespoon olive oil

3 large carrots, peeled and grated into long strips

1 teaspoon raw honey

½ teaspoon freshly squeezed lime juice

½ teaspoon kosher salt

MOROCCAN MINT GREEN TEA REDUCTION SAUCE

2 cups Moroccan mint green tea, brewed

⅛ teaspoon kosher salt

½ teaspoon raw honey

1 bag (cut open) or ½ tablespoon coarsely ground loose Moroccan mint green tea

1 tablespoon unsalted butter

TEA TOAST

8 to 10 slices walnut bread, toasted

3 ounces goat cheese

MAKES 8 TO 10 TOASTS

TO MAKE THE LENTILS: Bring a 2-quart saucepan with the lentils, water, and tea to boil. Simmer the lentils, uncovered, for 18 to 20 minutes. Press on the bag to extract all steeped liquid; discard the bag.

TO MAKE THE CARROTS: Place a 2-quart fry pan over medium-low heat for 1 minute. Swirl in the oil to coat. Turn the carrots in the oil to lightly coat. Stir in the honey, lime juice, and salt. Cook for 10 minutes. Transfer the carrots to a plate. Increase the heat to high.

TO MAKE THE SAUCE: Pour the tea into the hot pan. Stir in the salt and honey. Scrape occasionally. Reduce the sauce to a quarter of its original amount, about 6 to 7 minutes. Stir in the coarsely ground tea and butter.

TO ASSEMBLE: Layer each toast with lentils, goat cheese, carrot curls, and sauce.

WHITE BEAN WALNUT SPREAD *with* ROASTED TOMATO TEA TOAST

Think of this white bean walnut spread as a stand-in for all the ways you eat hummus. The Lapsang Souchong Salt will be what you reach for from now on in your everyday cooking to impart a slight smokiness.

MAKES 10 TOASTS

LAPSANG SOUCHONG SALT

⅓ cup kosher salt

2 tablespoons loose or 4 bags (cut open) lapsang souchong tea

ROASTED TOMATOES

7 to 8 small Campari tomatoes (tomatoes on the vine), sliced

1 tablespoon olive oil

¼ teaspoon Lapsang Souchong Salt

WHITE BEAN WALNUT SPREAD

1 (15-ounce) can cannellini white beans, drained and rinsed

½ cup toasted walnuts

1 medium clove garlic, minced

Juice of 1 lemon (3 tablespoons)

½ teaspoon loose lapsang souchong tea, finely ground

1 teaspoon Lapsang Souchong Salt

⅛ teaspoon freshly ground black pepper

¼ cup olive oil

TEA TOAST

1 loaf olive bread, sliced and toasted (may substitute wheat bread)

½ small bunch of chives

TO MAKE THE SALT: If using loose tea, grind the salt and tea together with a mortar and pestle or in a spice grinder until fine. If using tea bags, mix the tea and salt to combine. Store in a glass jar.

TO MAKE THE TOMATOES: Preheat the oven to 400°F. Line a 13 by 9-inch sheet pan with parchment paper and lay down the tomato slices. Brush each slice with oil and sprinkle with salt. Roast 20 minutes or until golden and wrinkled. Cool 5 minutes.

TO MAKE THE SPREAD: Purée the beans, walnuts, garlic, lemon juice, tea powder, Lapsang Souchong Salt, and black pepper in a food processor, drizzling in the oil while the machine is working.

TO ASSEMBLE: Heartily smear each toast with the spread and top with three tomato slices and snipped chives.

HURRICANE POPCORN
with TEA FURIKAKE

Popular in Hawaii, hurricane popcorn also has leagues of fans on the mainland. This tea version swaps out seaweed furikake for nutty Dragon Well. Make sure to pick through the tea for any twigs before grinding.

1 tablespoon loose Dragon Well tea, coarsely ground

1 teaspoon toasted sesame seeds

¼ teaspoon kosher salt

½ teaspoon sugar

¼ cup organic popcorn kernels

1 teaspoon safflower, grapeseed, or other neutral oil

MAKES 2 TO 4 SERVINGS

Stir the tea, sesame seeds, salt, and sugar in a bowl to make the furikake. Pop the corn by your preferred method, in a hot air popper or on the stovetop. Pour into a bowl. Drizzle with the oil and sprinkle on the furikake.

TEA CRACKERS *with* HERBED LABNEH

Labneh is often finished with a drizzle of olive oil and sprinkling of za'atar; in this recipe we stir in these spices. The herbed labneh is also used in Creamy Cucumber Roll-Ups (page 47).

MAKES ABOUT 90 CRACKERS AND 4 CUPS OF LABNEH

HERBED LABNEH (YOGURT CHEESE)

4 cups labneh

3 bags or 1½ tablespoons loose Moroccan mint green tea, coarsely ground

¼ teaspoon Lemon Powder (page 6) or lemon zest

1 teaspoon garlic powder

1 teaspoon salt

⅛ teaspoon freshly ground black pepper

TEA CRACKERS

1 cup (136 grams) spelt flour

½ cup (70 grams) all-purpose flour

1 tablespoon loose Dragon Well tea, coarsely ground

½ teaspoon dried chives

¼ teaspoon dried parsley

¼ teaspoon garlic powder

¾ teaspoon kosher salt

¼ cup olive oil

½ cup lapsang souchong tea, brewed and cooled (1 bag or ½ tablespoon loose)

TO MAKE THE LABNEH: Stir together the labneh, ground tea, lemon powder, garlic powder, salt, and pepper in a quart-sized glass jar. Cover and refrigerate. Use in two hours to one week.

TO MAKE THE CRACKERS: Preheat the oven to 400°F. Line an 18-inch sheet pan with parchment paper. Combine the flours, ground Dragon Well, chives, parsley, garlic powder, and salt. Mix in the oil and brewed tea until the dough comes together. Form into a ball and wrap in plastic wrap to rest for 10 minutes.

Lightly flour a work surface. Unwrap the ball and halve it, rewrapping the second half. Flour a rolling pin and roll the dough into a rectangle about ⅛ inch thick. (If the dough springs back, cover and rest it for a bit longer.) Use a pizza cutter to slice 1-inch squares, trimming uneven edges.

Lay the squares on the pan closely together but not touching. Stab each with a fork three times. Bake 12 minutes or until golden brown, turning the pan once halfway during baking. Cool. Repeat with the remaining dough. Store in a covered container.

NEW ORLEANS ICED TEA

For tea lovers, the smoky notes of lapsang souchong offer an alternative to New Orleans' distinctive chicory coffee. Over ice with a splash of half-and-half and vanilla simple syrup, this is my drink when I'm dreaming of the Big Easy.

½ cup water

½ cup sugar

1 teaspoon vanilla extract

4 cups lapsang souchong tea, brewed and cooled (¾ cup loose, coarsely ground)

1 cup ice, plus more for serving

4 to 6 tablespoons half-and-half

MAKES 4 TO 6 SERVINGS

TO MAKE THE VANILLA SIMPLE SYRUP: Pour the water and sugar in a 2-quart saucepan and set over high heat for 3 to 4 minutes, until the sugar dissolves. Turn off the heat. Stir in the vanilla extract. Cool.

TO SERVE: Pour the tea and simple syrup into a pitcher. Stir in 1 cup of ice until dissolved.

For each serving, pour 1 cup sweetened iced tea over ½ cup of ice in a tall glass. Stir in half-and-half to taste. Serve immediately.

WATERMELON TEA FRESCA

My friend Tyler can pull people and parties together with little fanfare and stir up a delectable *agua fresca* from almost any fruit. This tea fresca builds upon his party starters, with the added personality of English breakfast. I use Numi Tea's blend here, as it pairs well with watermelon.

½ cup sugar

½ cup water

2 pounds seedless watermelon, peeled and chopped

2¼ cups English breakfast tea, brewed and cooled (8 bags or ¼ cup loose)

1 cup water

MAKES 4 TO 6 SERVINGS

TO MAKE THE SIMPLE SYRUP: Pour the water and sugar in a 2-quart saucepan and set over high heat for 3 to 4 minutes, until the sugar dissolves. Turn off the heat. Cool.

TO MAKE THE FRESCA: Purée the watermelon in a blender until smooth. Strain through a fine-mesh sieve. Press on the solids to extract all the juice. Stir together the juice, tea, simple syrup, and 1 cup water. Serve over ice.

FORBIDDEN CHAI HORCHATA

This horchata surprises with its unexpected color, which comes from the black rice. According to legend, in ancient times only emperors in China could eat it—thus the name. Forbidden rice is found in natural food or specialty stores, but this recipe works just as well with regular white rice.

1 cup forbidden black rice
(or white rice)

2 cups water, at room temperature

6 cups masala chai tea, brewed and
cooled (4 bags or 2 tablespoons
loose)

1 cinnamon stick

½ cup Simple Syrup (page 40)

MAKES 4 TO 6 SERVINGS

Measure the rice into a medium bowl and pour the room-temperature water over it. Cover the bowl and leave on the counter to soak for 8 hours or overnight. Blend the horchata in two batches: Purée half each of the rice, soaking liquid, cinnamon stick, and tea in a blender for 2 minutes. Repeat. Strain the horchata through a fine-mesh sieve twice to remove any solid rice residue before pouring it into the serving pitcher. Stir in the simple syrup. Refrigerate and serve over ice.

HIGH TEA

SOUPS

Mint Pea Soup

Creamy Broccoli Soup

Smoky Tomato Soup with Parmesan Thyme Crisps

Chamomile Corn Chowder

Pumpkin Carrot Soup

SIDE DISHES

Orange-Jasmine Brussels Sprouts

Twice-Baked Garnet Yams with Chai Yogurt

Green Tea Coconut Rice

VEGETARIAN MAIN DISHES

Portobello Steak Frites

Cauliflower Steaks with Tea Umami Sauce

Black Bean Burgers with Green Tea Basil Aïoli

Swedish Mushroom "Meatballs" and Egg Noodles

Green Tea Noodles in Asparagus Sauce with Goat Cheese Pearls

PROVISION

Green Tea Stock

Now the day is over,
Night is drawing nigh,
Shadows of the evening
Steal across the sky.
— WILLIAM WORDSWORTH

Before you know it, the end of the day arrives.
This is the time of gathering around the table,
catching up, when the important stuff happens.
The family around you—whether by birth, marriage,
or the natural selection of friendship—are the people
who make life shimmer. Passing and sharing food
with them, the company of animal friends, the middle
of a good book—these are all elements of a rich life
indeed. Settle in at the table.

MINT PEA SOUP

Seattle and Portland may have their rain and New England its snow, but for most of the year, our fair block of San Francisco is thickly hemmed in with fog. Most days I relish the gray skies, but sometimes I wave a white flag of surrender. To drive away the doldrums, I make this vivid green soup, with Mighty Leaf Tea's Moroccan mint green tea substituting for broth.

1 tablespoon olive oil

1 medium white onion, chopped
  (1½ cups)

4 cups Moroccan mint green tea,
  brewed (8 bags or ¼ cup loose)

1 teaspoon Lapsang Souchong Salt
  (page 52)

½ teaspoon kosher salt

3½ cups frozen peas (1-pound package)
  or equivalent of fresh peas, shucked

¼ teaspoon Lemon Powder (page 6) or
  lemon zest

1 cup fresh spinach leaves

1 small clove garlic, minced
  (¼ teaspoon)

⅛ teaspoon ground black pepper

MAKES 4 TO 6 SERVINGS

Place an 8-quart stockpot over medium heat for 1 minute. Swirl the oil in the pot to coat. Sauté the onion for 5 minutes, stirring occasionally. Pour in the tea, and stir in the Lapsang Souchong Salt, kosher salt, peas, Lemon Powder or zest, and spinach. Turn the heat up. Cook for 5 minutes, until the pot is softly bubbling and the peas have cooked through. Stir in the minced garlic. Cool for 5 minutes. Purée in batches until smooth. Grind in black pepper to taste.

CREAMY BROCCOLI SOUP

In my household we eat soup with clockwork regularity, probably owing to the fact that we live in a chilly city. This broccoli soup owes its winsome flavor to two secrets: the tender, sweet inner heart of the broccoli stalk and the clean flavor of the Green Tea Stock (page 86).

1 large head broccoli

1 tablespoon olive oil

1 medium yellow onion, chopped
   (1 cup)

1 tablespoon unsalted butter

1 large russet potato, peeled and sliced
   into ¼-inch-thick rounds

1 teaspoon kosher salt

⅛ teaspoon ground black pepper

4 cups Green Tea Stock (page 86)

¼ teaspoon ground coriander

Parmesan cheese, for grating

MAKES 4 TO 6 SERVINGS

Chop off and reserve the broccoli florets. Peel and discard the woody bark from the broccoli stalks. Slice and reserve the inner broccoli hearts. Place an 8-quart stockpot over medium-low heat for 1 minute. Swirl in the oil to coat. Sauté the onion, stirring often, for 10 minutes or until translucent. Add the butter, potato, salt, and pepper, and sauté for 2 minutes. Pour in the stock and add the coriander. Bring to a boil. Reduce the heat to simmer, cover, and cook for 10 minutes. Add the broccoli hearts and florets; cover and cook until they are soft but not mushy, about 10 minutes. Purée or blend the soup until smooth or to desired texture. Serve with grated Parmesan.

SMOKY TOMATO SOUP *with* PARMESAN THYME CRISPS

My husband's eyes flicker at the mere mention of tomato soup with grilled cheese. So when the idea of adding tea fell on me, it felt like the apple tagging Newton. The elegant Parmesan thyme crisps concentrate cheese flavor into delectable morsels.

PARMESAN THYME CRISPS

½ cup shredded Parmesan

½ teaspoon thyme leaves
   (from 2 sprigs)

SMOKY TOMATO SOUP

1 tablespoon safflower, grapeseed, or
   other neutral oil

1 medium white onion, finely chopped
   (1 cup)

1 medium red bell pepper, peeled,
   roasted, and finely chopped (1 cup)

3 cups lapsang souchong tea, brewed
   (2 bags or 1 tablespoon loose)

1 cup water

1 (28-ounce) can whole peeled
   tomatoes (I use San Marzano),
   with the liquid

1 teaspoon kosher salt

⅛ teaspoon red pepper flakes

½ teaspoon dried thyme

MAKES 4 TO 6 SERVINGS

TO MAKE THE CRISPS: Preheat the oven to 275°F. Line a 13 by 9 by 1-inch sheet pan with parchment paper. Sprinkle shredded Parmesan in a thin, even layer on the pan. Polka dot the cheese with the thyme leaves. Bake for 18 minutes, or until the cheese is golden brown and baked through. Cool for about 10 minutes and snap into segments.

TO MAKE THE SOUP: Place an 8-quart stockpot over medium-low heat for 1 minute. Swirl in the oil to coat. Sauté the onion, stirring occasionally, for 5 minutes. Add the bell pepper and cook for 1 minute. Pour in the tea, water, and the liquid from the tomatoes. With your hands, break up the tomatoes over the pot and drop them in. Stir in the salt, red pepper flakes, and thyme. Turn the heat up to medium and cook, uncovered, for 10 minutes. Purée or blend until almost smooth with some chunks. Serve with Parmesan Thyme Crisps.

CHAMOMILE CORN CHOWDER

The floral honeyed tones of chamomile beautifully complement the sweetness of corn. This chowder owes its body to being half puréed, rather than to cream or butter, making it naturally vegan. I use frozen corn here, but if you're lucky enough to find fresh organic corn, by all means use it.

1 tablespoon safflower, grapeseed, or other neutral oil

1 medium white onion, chopped (1½ cups)

¼ medium green bell pepper, chopped (¼ cup)

4 small potatoes, chopped (1½ cups)

½ medium sweet potato, chopped (1 cup)

2 teaspoons kosher salt

Freshly ground black pepper

3½ cups chamomile tisane, brewed (4 bags or 2 tablespoons loose)

1 pound frozen organic corn kernels or the kernels from 2 ears of organic corn

2 tablespoons chopped fresh curly parsley

MAKES 2 TO 4 SERVINGS

Place an 8-quart stockpot over medium-low heat for 1 minute. Swirl the oil in the pot to coat. Sauté the onion and bell pepper for 5 minutes. Add the potatoes, sweet potato, salt, pepper, and chamomile. Raise the heat to medium-high. Once boiling, about 5 minutes, cover and lower the heat to simmer. Cook until the potatoes are fork-tender, about 5 minutes. Raise the heat to high. Stir in the corn and cook for 3 to 4 minutes.

Ladle half of the soup and solids into a blender, avoiding the sweet potato. Remove the cap from the blender lid and hold a towel over the opening. Purée until smooth. Return the puréed soup to the pot and stir to integrate. Grind in black pepper to taste. Garnish with the parsley.

PUMPKIN CARROT SOUP

French Provençal pumpkin entered my life through a farmer named Skip at my neighborhood farmers' market. This soup reminds me of fall mornings, jacket zipped and ready to bike off to discover what the day holds. If substituting canned pumpkin, forgo the roasting step and omit 1 tablespoon of the oil.

3 tablespoons olive oil

1 pound Provençal pumpkin, cut in half and seeded, or 1 cup canned pumpkin purée

3 cups rooibos, brewed (3 bags or 1½ tablespoons loose)

½-inch knob fresh ginger, peeled and minced (1 tablespoon)

1 medium red onion, chopped (1½ cups)

4 medium carrots, peeled and chopped into coins (2¼ cups)

1 tablespoon plus 1 teaspoon raw honey

½ teaspoon kosher salt

⅛ to ¼ teaspoon cayenne

1 tablespoon raw apple cider vinegar

MAKES 4 TO 5 SERVINGS

If using fresh pumpkin, preheat the oven to 400°F. Line an 18-inch sheet pan with parchment paper. Brush 1 tablespoon of the olive oil all over the pumpkin halves and roast for 1½ hours or until fork-tender. Cool the pumpkin. Scoop the flesh out in large chunks. Discard the skin.

Place an 8-quart stockpot over medium-low heat for 1 minute. Swirl in 1 tablespoon oil in the pot to coat. Sauté the ginger and onion for 5 minutes or until the onion is almost translucent. Add the remaining tablespoon of olive oil, carrots, honey, salt, and cayenne. Cook for 8 minutes. Stir in the pumpkin flesh or canned pumpkin purée and the rooibos. Bring to a boil. Cover the pot and lower the heat. Simmer for 15 minutes or until the carrots are fork-tender. Purée or blend smooth. Stir in the vinegar and serve.

ORANGE-JASMINE BRUSSELS SPROUTS

Like most children, I didn't care for Brussels sprouts. Like most adults, I circled back and reconsidered my position. These Orange-Jasmine Brussels Sprouts drive away the blues when spring seems on furlough.

14 Brussels sprouts, rinsed and chopped in half

1 teaspoon jasmine green tea powder (finely ground loose leaves or measured from a tea bag)

¼ teaspoon Sriracha

1 teaspoon raw honey

¼ teaspoon kosher salt

Pinch of freshly ground black pepper

1 tablespoon safflower, grapeseed, or other neutral oil

¼ cup orange juice, freshly squeezed

Zest of 1 medium orange

MAKES 2 TO 4 SERVINGS

Preheat the oven to 400°F. Line a 13 by 9-inch sheet pan with parchment paper. Place the Brussels sprouts in a bowl. Mix the tea powder, Sriracha, honey, salt, pepper, oil, orange juice, and orange zest to make an orange-jasmine glaze. Pour the glaze over the sprouts and toss to coat. Scatter the sprouts on the pan in a single layer flat-side down. Coat with any remaining glaze. Roast for 20 to 22 minutes, until browned.

TWICE-BAKED GARNET YAMS
with CHAI YOGURT

Chai-infused yogurt is worth the wait. Spoon it onto these twice-baked garnet yams, swirl it over warm brownies, or drizzle it on buckwheat pancakes. Aleppo pepper brings an unexpected note of tart mild heat.

MASALA CHAI YOGURT

½ cup plain whole milk yogurt (regular, not Greek style)

2 bags masala chai tea

TWICE-BAKED GARNET YAMS

3 medium garnet yams, rinsed and scrubbed

1 tablespoon unsalted butter

1 tablespoon mascarpone

Zest of 1 orange (1 tablespoon)

½ teaspoon kosher salt

⅛ teaspoon cayenne pepper

Pinch of freshly ground black pepper

3 chives, minced

Maldon sea salt

Aleppo pepper (optional)

MAKES 6 SERVINGS

TO MAKE THE YOGURT: Pour the yogurt into a glass jar and submerge the chai bags. Seal and chill the jar for 3 days, jostling it each day to distribute the tea. Press on the bags to extract all the steeped liquid, stirring it into the yogurt; discard the bags.

TO MAKE THE YAMS: Preheat the oven to 400°F and line an 18-inch sheet pan with parchment paper. Stab the yams a few times in the middle. Roast them for 1 hour and 20 minutes or until a fork pierces easily. Remove the yams (keep the oven on) and cut them lengthwise. Scoop the cooked yam centers into a bowl (reserve the shells). Mash the yam flesh with butter, mascarpone, zest, salt, cayenne, and black pepper. Fill the yam shells with the seasoned mashed yam flesh. Bake for 20 minutes.

TO SERVE: Top each yam half with a dollop of yogurt, sprinkle of minced chives, pinch of Maldon sea salt, and Aleppo pepper, if using.

GREEN TEA COCONUT RICE

This gorgeous green tea coconut rice stands up to Thai takeout and melds beautifully with sautéed eggplant. I wouldn't suggest swapping light coconut milk for the real deal—your rice would be left wanting that supple quality inherent in coconut rice. Choose a superb matcha green tea powder that is grassy and stark green—I used one from Steven Smith Teamaker. Basmati rice works with this recipe, but I prefer the texture of a long-grain.

2 cups long-grain white rice

1½ cups 175°F water

2 tablespoons matcha green tea powder

1 (13½-ounce) can coconut milk

MAKES 6 TO 8 SIDE SERVINGS

Rinse the rice twice and drain. Measure the matcha into a medium glass bowl. Pour in ¼ cup hot water and whisk vigorously for 1 minute, or until the tea is clump-free. Only then whisk in the remaining hot water. Pour the coconut milk and matcha tea into a 2-quart saucepan and put over high heat, stirring. When the surface bubbles, stir in the rice. Cover and turn the heat to low. Simmer for 20 minutes. Turn off the heat. Keep covered for 5 minutes before fluffing with a fork and serving.

Great lemons, cut in disks, would sink like suns into the golden dusk of the tea, dimly shining through it with the radiant flesh of their fruit.

—RAINER MARIA RILKE

PORTOBELLO STEAK FRITES

This meal is a fun bit of tongue-in-cheek. The "steak" is portobello, and the "frites" are polenta strips. (You can skip the baking and serve the polenta straight.) Both tisane and tea are used: Chamomile enhances the polenta's corn flavor, and lapsang souchong poaches a suggestion of smokiness into the portobello.

MAKES 4 SERVINGS

PORTOBELLO STEAKS AU POIVRE

2 tablespoons Dijon mustard

1 tablespoon liquid aminos or organic soy sauce

2 tablespoons fresh lemon juice

2 teaspoons dried chives

½ cup olive oil

4 portobello mushroom caps

1 cup lapsang souchong tea, brewed (2 bags or 1 tablespoon loose)

1 tablespoon black peppercorns, coarsely ground

2 large shallots, peeled and sliced (¼ cup)

¼ teaspoon kosher salt

BAKED POLENTA FRITES

4 cups chamomile tisane, brewed (6 bags or 3 tablespoons loose)

½ cup whole milk

1 teaspoon kosher salt

1 cup coarse-ground polenta or grits

¼ cup half-and-half

3 tablespoons unsalted butter, cubed

TO MARINATE THE MUSHROOM STEAKS: Whisk the mustard, liquid aminos, lemon juice, chives, and oil in a small bowl. Pull the stems from the mushroom caps and scrape out the gills with a spoon. Coat the caps in the marinade. Cover for 30 minutes.

TO MAKE THE POLENTA: If baking into frites, preheat the oven to 400°F and line an 18-inch sheet pan with parchment paper. Bring the chamomile tisane, milk, and salt to boil in a 2-quart saucepan. Stir in the polenta and lower the heat to simmer, stirring often for 15 minutes. Stir in the half-and-half and butter and cook 5 minutes. The polenta can be served at this stage. To make into frites, pour into an 8 by 8-inch pan and cool 15 minutes. Cut into 16 strips. Use a spatula to transfer them to the sheet pan, leaving space between. Bake 20 minutes or until crispy.

TO FINISH THE STEAKS: Scatter the pepper on a plate. Press the top of each mushroom cap onto the plate to embed the pepper. Pour the tea into a 2-quart fry pan with the shallots and salt. Bring to a boil. Place the mushrooms in the pan topside down and turn the heat to low. Cover and steam 10 minutes. Carefully remove the steaks, flip, and serve.

CAULIFLOWER STEAKS *with* TEA UMAMI SAUCE

My impulse visit to Blue Hill in New York City left an indelible imprint. The crown jewel—surpassing even the dessert course—involved a cauliflower steak the size of a dinner plate, crisped on the edges and luscious under the weight of my fork. This recipe is my homage to that evening.

CAULIFLOWER STEAKS

2 heads cauliflower, rinsed and patted dry, sliced into 4 steaks 1½ inch thick

4 tablespoons safflower, grapeseed, or other neutral oil

TEA UMAMI SAUCE

¼ cup lapsang souchong tea, brewed and cooled (1 teaspoon loose, finely ground)

¼ cup tahini

1 tablespoon liquid aminos or organic soy sauce

1 tablespoon maple syrup

⅛ teaspoon coarsely ground black pepper

Sumac, for garnish (optional)

2 tablespoons chopped fresh parsley, for garnish (optional)

MAKES 4 SERVINGS

TO MAKE THE CAULIFLOWER STEAKS: Place an 18-inch sheet pan on the middle oven rack. Preheat to 450°F. Position a foil tent on a plate near the stove.

Place a 2-quart fry pan over medium-high heat for 1 minute. Swirl in 2 tablespoons oil to coat. When the pan begins smoking, use tongs to carefully place (it may splatter) one steak in the hot oil. Sear 2 minutes. Turn and sear the flip side 2 minutes. Transfer the steak to the plate and cover with the foil tent. Repeat with the other steaks, adding oil as needed.

Once all the steaks have cooked, arrange them on the preheated sheet pan, making sure no sides are touching. Bake 10 minutes.

TO SERVE: Whisk the tea with the tahini, liquid aminos, maple syrup, and pepper. Pour the umami sauce over the steaks. Sprinkle with sumac and chopped parsley, if using.

BLACK BEAN BURGERS *with* GREEN TEA BASIL AÏOLI

Toasted pecans are the key to these black bean beauties, along with the matcha in the piquant aïoli.

BLACK BEAN BURGERS

1 tablespoon olive oil

1 small carrot, shredded (½ cup)

½ medium green bell pepper, seeded and finely chopped (½ cup)

1 medium red onion, finely chopped (1 cup)

1 large clove garlic, minced

1 teaspoon kosher salt

2 (15-ounce) cans black beans

½ cup toasted pecans

2 eggs

½ cup dry breadcrumbs

½ teaspoon red pepper flakes

GREEN TEA BASIL AÏOLI

4 cloves garlic

10 large fresh basil leaves

3 teaspoons matcha green tea powder

4 egg yolks

4 teaspoons freshly squeezed lemon juice

1 teaspoon Dijon mustard

½ cup olive oil

MAKES 6 TO 8 BURGERS

TO MAKE THE BURGERS: Preheat the oven to 350°F. Line an 18-inch sheet pan with parchment paper. Place a 2-quart fry pan over medium-low heat for 1 minute. Swirl in the oil to coat. Sauté the carrot, bell pepper, onion, garlic, and salt for about 8 minutes, or until the onion is translucent. Turn off the heat. Drain both cans of beans. Pour one can into a large bowl. Pour the other into a food processor with the pecans, bell pepper, onion, and garlic and pulse to a coarse paste. Add to the whole beans. Mix in the eggs, breadcrumbs, and red pepper flakes. Mound ½-cup patties onto the baking sheet, pressing lightly to flatten. Leave a ½ inch between patties. Bake 45 minutes until dry and a bit crisp.

TO MAKE THE AÏOLI: Purée the garlic, basil, matcha, yolks, lemon juice, mustard, and salt and pepper to taste with a blender or food processor. Add the oil in a slow stream until smooth.

Serve as you like: I put them on whole wheat buns smeared with aïoli and dressed with lettuce and tomato.

SWEDISH MUSHROOM "MEATBALLS" *and* EGG NOODLES

Meatless Swedish meatballs in mushroom sauce make a mighty comforting meal. Serve this dish on a cold evening to rekindle and stoke your internal fire.

MAKES 3 TO 4 SERVINGS

MUSHROOM "MEATBALLS"

¼ cup cooked steel-cut oats

1 (15-ounce) can cannellini beans, drained and rinsed

2 teaspoons olive oil

2 shallots, minced (3 tablespoons)

6 button mushrooms, minced (1½ cups)

¾ teaspoon kosher salt

¼ teaspoon minced fresh rosemary

1 tablespoon minced fresh parsley

¼ teaspoon freshly cracked black pepper

¼ teaspoon loose lapsang souchong tea, finely ground or from 1 bag (cut open)

½ cup fresh breadcrumbs

2 eggs

MUSHROOM SAUCE

2 tablespoons olive oil, divided

2 shallots, minced (3 tablespoons)

12 button mushrooms, sliced (2½ cups)

⅛ teaspoon loose lapsang souchong tea, finely ground or from 1 bag (cut open)

¾ teaspoon kosher salt

1 teaspoon sherry (may substitute white wine)

2 tablespoons all-purpose flour

1½ cups whole milk

3 tablespoons plain kefir

¼ teaspoon freshly ground black pepper

1 (16-ounce) package egg noodles

Chopped parsley, for garnish

TO MAKE THE MEATBALLS: Preheat the oven to 350°F. Line an 18-inch sheet pan with parchment paper. Pulse the cooked oatmeal and beans in a food processor until integrated, about 15 seconds, or mash with a potato masher. Transfer to a medium bowl.

Set a 2-quart fry pan over medium heat for 1 minute. Swirl in the oil to coat. Sauté the shallots, mushrooms, salt, and rosemary for 3 minutes. Cool for 5 minutes and transfer to the bowl with the bean mixture. Stir in the parsley, pepper, ground tea, bread-crumbs, and eggs until integrated.

Scoop the meatballs with a tablespoon onto the sheet pan an inch apart. Bake 45 minutes or until browned.

TO MAKE THE MUSHROOM SAUCE: Set a 2-quart fry pan over medium-low heat for 1 minute. Swirl in 1 tablespoon of the oil to coat. Sauté the shallots 4 minutes or until translucent. Add the remaining tablespoon oil, mushrooms, finely ground tea, and salt and cook 5 minutes. Pour in the sherry. Whisk in the flour briskly, making sure it doesn't clump. Whisk in the milk. Turn the heat down to low and simmer over low heat about 15 minutes, or until the sauce cooks down and thickens, whisking occasionally. Turn off the heat. Stir in the kefir and pepper.

While the sauce cooks, prepare the noodles according to pack-age instructions. Serve with meatballs, sauce, and parsley.

GREEN TEA NOODLES *in* ASPARAGUS SAUCE *with* GOAT CHEESE PEARLS

This fanciful dish resembles strands of green necklaces with goat cheese pearls. If you choose not to roll the goat cheese, crumble it instead. Hand-rolling pasta is not for the weak of arm; thus, this recipe is written for a pasta machine.

GREEN TEA NOODLES AND GOAT CHEESE PEARLS

1½ cups (204 grams) spelt flour

1½ cups (210 grams) all-purpose flour

½ teaspoon kosher salt

2 teaspoons matcha green tea powder

4 eggs at room temperature

2 tablespoons lukewarm water, optional

2 ounces goat cheese

ASPARAGUS SAUCE

1 bunch asparagus, chopped into
    ½ inch coins and steamed

Zest of 1 lemon (1 teaspoon)

2 small cloves garlic

1 teaspoon kosher salt

⅛ teaspoon freshly ground black pepper

½ cup parsley leaves

½ cup olive oil

½ cup pasta water

MAKES 4 TO 6 SERVINGS

TO MAKE THE NOODLES: Stir together the flours, salt, and tea. Break the eggs into a well in the flour and whisk them. With your hands, mix the flour and eggs. If needed, add the water, 1 tablespoon at a time, until the dough just comes together but is not sticky. Knead until it forms a ball. Turn the ball onto a lightly floured surface. Knead again until firm—it will resist and spring back. Wrap in plastic wrap and rest it for 30 to 45 minutes or until a finger indentation does not spring back.

Meanwhile, pinch off pieces of goat cheese and roll in your palms. Put the pearls in a pan large enough that they don't touch each other (a shallow Pyrex baking pan with lid is ideal). Cover and refrigerate.

Flour a large bowl and position the bowl on a chair near the pasta machine. This is to catch the noodles. Unwrap and halve the dough ball, rewrapping the second half. Press the dough into a rectangle. Lightly flour both sides. Nudge the dough into the machine and roll two times through on the thickest setting, lightly flouring as needed. Turn the roller down to the median setting and feed the sheet through. Finally, run the sheet through the linguine cutter, letting the strands fall into the waiting bowl. Toss in the flour so they don't clump. Repeat with the remaining dough.

(CONTINUED)

GREEN TEA NOODLES *in* ASPARAGUS SAUCE *with* GOAT CHEESE PEARLS

(CONTINUED)

Fill an 8-quart stockpot three-quarters full of water, cover, and bring to a boil. Cook the noodles 6 minutes or until al dente. Drain them, reserving ½ cup of the pasta water for the sauce.

TO MAKE THE ASPARAGUS SAUCE: Purée the asparagus with the lemon zest, garlic, salt, pepper, parsley, and oil until smooth. Pour the sauce into a 2-quart saucepan. Stir in the reserved pasta water and heat through. Toss the noodles and sauce. Garnish with the goat cheese pearls.

GREEN TEA STOCK

This green tea stock can be used right away to make Creamy Broccoli Soup (page 64) or kept in the freezer to give a boost to ordinary recipes. It can even be soothing to sip on its own if you're unwell. Select a Dragon Well green tea with flat, full whole leaves, like the ones from the Tao of Tea or Silk Road Teas.

1 tablespoon olive oil

1 large white onion, chopped
   (1½ cups)

1 large celery stalk, chopped (½ cup)

4 small carrots, peeled and chopped
   (1¼ cup)

2 teaspoons kosher salt

⅛ teaspoon freshly ground black pepper

5 cups Dragon Well tea, brewed
   (10 bags or ⅓ cup loose)

MAKES 4 CUPS

Place an 8-quart stockpot over medium-low heat for 1 minute. Swirl in the oil to coat. Sauté the onions for 3 minutes, stirring occasionally. Add the celery and carrots and sauté for 3 minutes, stirring occasionally. Stir in the salt and pepper. Pour in the tea and bring to a boil. Cover and reduce the heat. Simmer the stock for 30 minutes, and strain through a fine-mesh sieve. Press on the onions, celery, and carrots to extract all the steeped liquid; discard the vegetables. The stock can be stored in the freezer for 4 to 6 months. Pour into ice cube trays—rectangular ice cube wells hold 2 tablespoons, perfect for adding smaller amounts to recipes. Or store in quart-sized jars or freezer-safe resealable bags.

SWEET TEA

COMFORT

Chamomile Risotto with Currants

Earl Grey Poached Pears with Masala Chai Caramel Sauce

BAKED

Green Tea Sesame Shortbread Cookies

Mini Cherry Chai Cream Pies with Sweet Tea Glaze

Jasmine Cacao Nib Meringues

Mary Sue's Iced Tea Sugar Cookies

Spelt Shortcakes with Cantaloupe and Jasmine Whipped Cream

Evelyn's English Breakfast Meringue–Frosted Chocolate Bar Cake

COLD

Rooibos Red Fruit Kanten

Chamomile Buttermilk Pudding with Caramelized Banana

Pistachio Panna Cotta with Chocolate Matcha Crunch Clusters

Chocolate Earl Grey Custard with Candied Kumquats

Salted Almond Ice Cream with Masala Magic Sauce

Chai Frozen Hot Chocolate Malts

Matcha Teaffogato with Toasted Coconut Ice Cream

Toasted Pecan Paletas

Hard Cider Floats with Maple Chai Ice Cream

PROVISION

Jasmine Tea Extract

LAST BITE

Bittersweet Moroccan Mint Truffles

Something about evening brings with it sweetness. Nighttime comes as a reprieve, the time of after-dinner mints or herbal tisanes to warm chilly nights. Dessert might be vilified in some circles, but not here, not tonight. In deepest darkness is when we discern the spectacular smattering of stars pinpricking the sky. Linger over the last drops of the evening.

If it's darkness we're having,
let it be extravagant.

—JANE KENYON

CHAMOMILE RISOTTO *with* CURRANTS

Rice pudding is quite the international dish. My Mexican mother craves *arroz con leche* with cinnamon and raisins. In India, *kheer* is scented with cardamom. Italy bakes their version in *budino di riso*. This version simmers Arborio rice in a floral chamomile broth rather than milk.

1 tablespoon unsalted butter

1½ cups Arborio rice

⅓ cup sugar

¼ teaspoon kosher salt

5 cups chamomile tisane, brewed
    (6 bags or 5 tablespoons loose)

2 tablespoons dried currants

MAKES 4 TO 6 SERVINGS

Place a 2-quart saucepan over medium-low heat. Melt the butter into the saucepan. Stir the rice into the butter to coat. Add the sugar and salt. Pour ¾ cup of the chamomile into the pan and stir for 10 minutes or until the liquid has been absorbed. The risotto will take about an hour to cook, so expect to stir the pan and add ¾ cup chamomile at 10-minute intervals. As you near an hour, the risotto will thicken and become creamy. Turn off the heat. Stir in the currants.

EARL GREY POACHED PEARS *with* MASALA CHAI CARAMEL SAUCE

Be generous with the caramel sauce, friends. Making caramel requires alertness. When the color transition happens, it happens quickly, so have all the ingredients close by. Use a heavy-bottomed saucepan with tall sides and a long-handled spoon.

MASALA CHAI CARAMEL SAUCE

1 cup heavy cream

2 bags or 1 tablespoon loose masala chai tea

1 cup sugar

¾ teaspoon kosher salt

½ cup water

4 tablespoons unsalted butter, at room temperature

1 teaspoon Masala Chai Extract (page 112)

EARL GREY POACHED PEARS

3 Bartlett pears, peeled, cored, and halved

6 tablespoons sugar

½ teaspoon freshly squeezed lemon juice

7 cups water

¼ cup loose Earl Grey tea

MAKES 3 GENEROUS TO 6 SMALL SERVINGS

TO MAKE THE CARAMEL SAUCE: Bring the cream to a rolling boil in a 2-quart fry pan. Turn off the heat. Plunge the tea into the cream. Steep for 10 minutes. Strain the tea through a fine-mesh sieve if using loose. Press on the bags or leaves to extract all the steeped liquid; discard the bags or leaves. Pour the sugar and salt into the middle of a 2-quart saucepan. Pour the water over the sugar, making sure it is submerged. Bring to a boil over high heat. Do not stir.

Watch carefully! It will bubble and roil. When the color changes from pale amber to deep amber tinged with red, pour in a small amount of cream. The mixture will writhe passionately; stir it down, then slowly stir in the remaining cream. Turn the heat to low and stir for a minute. Remove from heat. Stir in the butter and extract. Cool the sauce to room temperature.

TO MAKE THE PEARS: Meanwhile, put the pears, sugar, lemon juice, and water in a 2-quart saucepan. Bring to a boil. Stir in the tea. Lower the heat and cover the saucepan. Simmer for 12 to 15 minutes until a fork pierces easily. Remove from the heat. Transfer to serving bowls and drizzle with warm caramel sauce.

GREEN TEA SESAME SHORTBREAD COOKIES

I concocted this shortbread for a bake sale to raise donations for Japan after the terrible tsunami, and it has stayed in my collection. Substitute regular sesame seeds if you can't find black sesame seeds or omit them.

2 cups (272 grams) spelt flour

½ cup cornstarch

2 teaspoons matcha green tea powder

¼ teaspoon kosher salt

1 cup unsalted butter, at room temperature

½ cup sugar

3 tablespoons black sesame seeds

MAKES 20 COOKIES

Whisk the flour, cornstarch, matcha, and salt in a mixing bowl. Cream the butter and sugar on high in a stand mixer or with an electric hand mixer 2 minutes or until fluffy. Lower the speed to medium. Add the flour mixture gradually until combined and form into a ball.

Cover a work surface with a large sheet of parchment paper and put the dough ball in the center. Fold the parchment over the dough and massage and coax it to lengthen. Once it is lengthened into a log, open the parchment and distribute the sesame seeds below and above the log. Roll the log over the seeds so they embed in the sides. Roll the parchment tightly and twist the ends.

Refrigerate at least an hour or overnight. When ready to bake, preheat the oven to 275°F. Line an 18-inch sheet pan with parchment paper. Cut ½-inch slices from the log and set them 1-inch apart on the pan. Bake 30 minutes or until golden.

MINI CHERRY CHAI CREAM PIES
with SWEET TEA GLAZE

To make the masala chai and English breakfast sugars, respectively, combine ½ tablespoon loose, finely ground or 1 bag (cut open) tea with ½ cup of sugar in a jar. Seal and jostle the jar. I baked my pies in two 1¾-inch mini muffin pans. If using regular muffin pans, cut your crusts accordingly and double the pastry cream and cherries.

CHAI PASTRY CREAM

1 cup heavy cream

½ cup whole milk

⅓ cup masala chai sugar
    (see introductory note)

⅛ teaspoon kosher salt

3 egg yolks

2 tablespoons cornstarch

BLACK TEA PIE CRUST

1 cup (140 grams) all-purpose flour

¼ cup (34 grams) spelt flour

¼ teaspoon kosher salt

1 tablespoon English breakfast sugar
    (see introductory note)

8 tablespoons unsalted butter,
    cold and cubed

4 to 6 tablespoons water, cold

MINI PIES

¼ cup Sweet Tea Jelly (page 19)

1 tablespoon water

12 cherries, stemmed, pitted, and halved

MAKES 24 MINI PIES OR 10 REGULAR MUFFIN-SIZED PIES

TO MAKE THE CHAI PASTRY CREAM: Pour the cream, milk, chai sugar, and salt into a 2-quart saucepan over medium heat. Stir occasionally. Once the sugar dissolves, about 3 minutes, remove from the heat.

In a medium bowl, whisk the yolks and cornstarch into a yellow paste. Whisk in ¼ cup of the hot cream. Whisk constantly while slowly pouring in the remaining cream. Pour the custard back into the saucepan and place it over medium-low heat. Whisk constantly for 2 to 3 minutes, until it thickens and the whisk leaves drag marks.

Remove from the heat. Stir and strain through a fine-mesh sieve into a small bowl. Place a piece of plastic wrap directly onto the pastry cream surface. Refrigerate until cold, about 3 hours.

TO MAKE THE PIE CRUST: Stir the flours, salt, and English breakfast sugar in a large bowl. Using your fingers, rub the butter cubes into the flour until combined and pea-sized. Mix in the cold water until the dough coheres. Form the dough into a ball, wrap it in plastic wrap, and refrigerate 30 minutes, or until firm as a baseball.

(CONTINUED)

MINI CHERRY CHAI CREAM PIES
with SWEET TEA GLAZE

(CONTINUED)

Flour a work surface, your hands, and a rolling pin. Roll from the middle of the dough out away from you and rotate the dough. Roll and rotate until the dough is ⅛ inch thick.

Cut the dough into 2-inch-wide strips (or whatever spans your muffin wells). Drape the strip over one row of muffin wells. Flour a tart tamper or your fingers and nudge the dough into each well. Trim to fit. Refrigerate 30 minutes. When the dough is chilled, it is ready to bake.

Preheat the oven to 425°F. Cut one aluminum foil square per pie, sized about 50 percent larger than the diameter (for my 1¾-inch mini muffin wells, 3 by 3-inch was perfect). Fit the foil into the crust. Mound pie weights, uncooked rice, or dried beans into the foiled wells. Bake for 15 minutes. Pull the pans from the oven and remove the pie beans and foil squares. Return the pans to the oven and bake 3 to 5 minutes more. Cool 20 minutes.

TO ASSEMBLE: Stir the jelly and water in a small skillet over low heat until warm and combined. Turn off the heat. Fill a pastry bag (or a ziplock bag with a ¼-inch hole snipped from one corner) with the chilled pastry cream. Fill each crust with cream. Top with half a cherry. Brush the glaze on the cherries. The pies taste best the day they are made.

JASMINE CACAO NIB MERINGUES

Meringues make any occasion special. Jasmine scents these light-as-air morsels that are flecked with whispers of chocolate. Since meringues soak up moisture in the air, make them on dry days, as meringues may weep in humid weather, and then you may, too. And remember, when life gives you leftover yolks, make Lemon Curd (page 25).

4 egg whites, at room temperature

1 cup sugar

1 teaspoon Jasmine Tea Extract
  (page 112)

⅛ teaspoon kosher salt

1 tablespoon plus 1 teaspoon
  raw cacao nibs

MAKES 12 MERINGUES

Preheat the oven to 200°F. Line two 13 by 9-inch sheet pans with parchment paper. Fit the whisk attachment onto a stand mixer or use a handheld electric mixer. Beat the egg whites, starting on low and increasing to high, until thick and foamy.

Mix in the sugar, 1 tablespoon at first, then more as you go. Add the extract and salt. Beat the whites until they are in the stiff peak stage: firm with stiff spikes that hold their shape. Whisk in the cacao nibs.

Portion out the meringues using two spoons or a ¼-cup measuring cup and a spoon. Space the meringues 2 inches apart on the pans. Bake 3 hours or until the outsides stiffen and are not tacky. The meringues should easily lift from the parchment. Cool on the pans 20 minutes before serving. Store in a sealed container for up to one week.

MARY SUE'S ICED TEA SUGAR COOKIES

Mary Sue makes the best iced sugar cookies in Dallas. I added spelt to her recipe for a bit of whole grain body, and created six iced tea glazes to give options for all tea and tisane preferences. Each glaze recipe makes enough for one batch of dough, so multiply the recipe accordingly to serve a selection of glazes.

SUGAR COOKIES

1 cup (136 grams) spelt flour

1½ cups (210 grams) all-purpose flour

1 cup unsalted butter, at room temperature

⅔ cup sugar

1 egg

½ teaspoon kosher salt

LEMON TEA GLAZE

1 cup confectioners' sugar

2 tablespoons English breakfast tea, brewed and cooled (1 bag or 1 teaspoon loose)

⅛ teaspoon lemon zest

MAKES 24 COOKIES, DEPENDING ON SIZE

TO MAKE THE COOKIES: Stir the flours in a large bowl. Fit a stand mixer with the paddle attachment or use an electric hand mixer. Beat the butter and sugar 2 minutes until fluffy. Add the egg and beat 1 minute. Gradually add the flour and salt until just well mixed. Form the dough into a ball and wrap in plastic wrap. Refrigerate 2 hours.

Preheat the oven to 325°F. Line two 18-inch sheet pans with parchment paper. Flour a work surface and rolling pin. Press down lightly on the dough and roll from the middle out. Rotate and roll until the dough is ¼ inch thick, reflouring the rolling pin as needed. Cut out cookies and place them on the pans with ½ inch between. Bake 12 to 15 minutes, until golden brown.

TO MAKE THE GLAZE: Sift the confectioners' sugar into a small bowl. Stir in tea and lemon zest.

FOR ALL GLAZES: Paint onto the cooled cookies with a pastry brush. Let the glaze harden before serving.

OTHER ICED TEA GLAZES Follow the recipe for Lemon Tea
Glaze but substitute the following for the English breakfast
and lemon zest:

EARL GREY GLAZE

2 tablespoons Earl Grey tea, brewed and cooled,
and ⅛ teaspoon grapefruit or orange zest, grated

MASALA CHAI GLAZE

2 tablespoons masala chai tea, brewed and cooled,
and ⅛ teaspoon ginger, grated

MATCHA GLAZE

2 tablespoons matcha green tea, brewed and cooled

MOJITO GLAZE

2 tablespoons Moroccan mint green tea, brewed and cooled,
and ⅛ teaspoon lime zest

ROOIBOS CARROT GLAZE

2 tablespoons rooibos tisane, brewed and cooled,
and ⅛ teaspoon carrot, finely grated

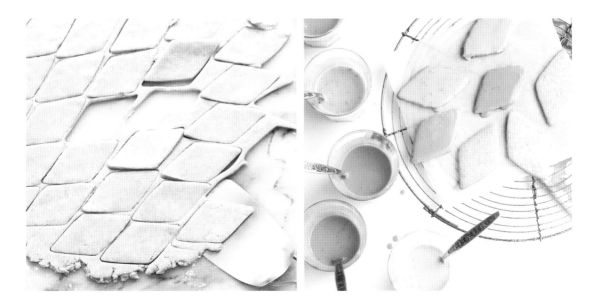

SPELT SHORTCAKES *with* CANTALOUPE *and* JASMINE WHIPPED CREAM

Shelve the strawberry shortcake, and make way for this one topped with sweet juicy cantaloupe. Jasmine Tea Extract (page 112) imparts a subtle floral note to the whipped cream, which is also wonderful on berries or flourless chocolate cake. Omit the sugar in the shortcakes to serve them with Chamomile Corn Chowder (page 66).

SPELT SHORTCAKES

1 cup (140 grams) all-purpose flour

1 cup (136 grams) spelt flour

½ teaspoon kosher salt

2 tablespoons sugar

2 teaspoons baking powder

8 tablespoons unsalted butter, cubed and chilled in the freezer for 10 minutes

1 cup heavy cream

JASMINE WHIPPED CREAM

1 cup heavy cream

2 teaspoons Jasmine Tea Extract (page 112)

1 tablespoon sugar

1 cup cantaloupe, diced

MAKES 5 TO 6 SERVINGS

TO MAKE THE SHORTCAKES: Preheat the oven to 400°F. Whisk the flours, salt, sugar, and baking powder in a mixing bowl. Cut the butter into the flour with a pastry cutter or two knives until pea-sized. Pour in the cream and stir until shaggy. Do not overmix. Gather the dough into a ball.

Flour a work surface, your hands, and a rolling pin and move the dough to the surface. Lightly roll the dough from the middle away from you. Rotate and roll until the dough is 1 inch thick.

Flour a biscuit cutter or cookie cutter and stamp out rounds close together, pressing down all the way. Gather and roll the scraps to cut out the remaining shortcakes. Place 2 inches apart on a 13 by 9-inch sheet pan. Bake 22 minutes, or until lightly browned or a toothpick comes out clean.

TO MAKE THE WHIPPED CREAM: Refrigerate a bowl and beaters until cold. Whip the cream until soft peaks form. Add the extract and sugar, beating until stiff peaks form.

Top the split shortcakes with cantaloupe and whipped cream.

EVELYN'S ENGLISH BREAKFAST MERINGUE–FROSTED CHOCOLATE BAR CAKE

We all need a ringer recipe. Yvonne, my mother-in-law, got this recipe from her mom, Evelyn, and now it's been handed down to me. My addition is the English breakfast meringue. The frosting will crack and the middle will fall. Rest assured, looks don't matter—this is a cake that makes friends.

1½ cups (210 grams) all-purpose flour

¼ cup (34 grams) spelt flour

1¾ teaspoons baking powder

¾ teaspoon kosher salt

1 cup cold unsalted butter

½ cup sugar

½ cup brown sugar

3 egg yolks

2 teaspoons English Breakfast Extract (page 112)

3½ ounces bittersweet chocolate bar, chopped (½ cup)

ENGLISH BREAKFAST MERINGUE

3 egg whites, room temperature

1 cup brown sugar

2 teaspoons English Breakfast Extract (page 112)

MAKES 12 TO 14 SLICES

TO MAKE THE CAKE: Preheat the oven to 325°F. Grease a 9-inch round pan and line the bottom with parchment paper. Whisk the flours with the baking powder, baking soda, and salt. Fit a stand mixer with the paddle attachment or use an electric hand mixer. Beat the butter, sugar, and brown sugar for 5 minutes. Beat in the yolks one at a time. Add the extract. Turn the speed to medium and mix the dry ingredients into the creamed butter until just combined. Spread the batter evenly in the pan. Scatter the chocolate on top. Set the cake aside while you make the meringue.

TO MAKE THE MERINGUE: Wash and dry the mixer bowl. Fit the mixer with the whisk attachment. Beat the egg whites, starting on low and increasing to high, until thick and voluminous. Mix in the brown sugar, 1 tablespoon at first, then more as you go. Once soft peaks form, add the extract. Spread the meringue evenly over the top of the cake. Bake for 1 hour and 10 minutes. Cool 30 minutes.

ROOIBOS RED FRUIT KANTEN

The vegetarian algae thickener known as agar agar also goes by the name kanten. Either way, it works like gelatin. Make this sophisticated cooling sweet in glass ramekins or juice glasses to show off the colors and enjoy it on hot summer evenings.

18 raspberries

6 strawberries, hulled and chopped

12 cherries, stemmed, pitted, and quartered

3 cups rooibos, brewed 10 minutes to concentrate (8 bags or ¼ cup loose)

¼ cup sugar

1 teaspoon vanilla extract

½ teaspoon fresh lemon juice

3 tablespoons agar agar

MAKES 6 SERVINGS

Set out six 6-ounce glasses. Place the following into each: three raspberries, one chopped strawberry, and two quartered cherries. Stir the rooibos, sugar, vanilla extract, lemon juice, and agar agar in a 2-quart saucepan. Bring to a boil over high heat, then lower the heat to simmer 5 minutes. Stir occasionally to ensure that nothing sticks to the bottom. Turn off the heat. Carefully ladle ¼ cup into each glass. Gently stir in any fruit that bobs to the top. Cover and refrigerate 2 hours, or until cold and solid.

CHAMOMILE BUTTERMILK PUDDING
with CARAMELIZED BANANA

This luscious chamomile version of banana pudding gets an edge from tart buttermilk and glamour from caramelized banana.

CHAMOMILE BUTTERMILK PUDDING

1 cup heavy cream

1 cup buttermilk

1 cup whole milk

½ cup Chamomile Sugar (page 27)

½ tablespoon crushed chamomile petals, loose or from 1 bag (cut open)

¼ teaspoon kosher salt

3 egg yolks

5 teaspoons cornstarch

CARAMELIZED BANANA

1 tablespoon unsalted butter

1 tablespoon brown sugar

⅛ teaspoon kosher salt

1 banana, peeled and diagonally sliced into 4 long ovals

MAKES 4 SERVINGS

TO MAKE THE PUDDING: Pour the cream, buttermilk, and milk into a 2-quart saucepan placed over medium heat. Stir in the chamomile sugar, chamomile petals, and salt and cook about 5 minutes or until the sugar dissolves, stirring occasionally with a wooden spoon. Remove from the heat.

Whisk the yolks and cornstarch in a medium bowl to a yellow paste. Continue whisking while pouring ¼ cup chamomile cream into the yolks. Whisk constantly and gradually pour in the remaining hot cream until combined. Pour the pudding back into the saucepan. Whisk constantly over medium-low heat about 4 to 5 minutes or until it thickens and the whisk leaves drag marks. Remove the pot from the heat.

Strain the pudding through a fine-mesh sieve into a clean bowl, gently whisking to keep the pudding flowing. Cover the bowl and refrigerate 3 hours, or until chilled.

TO MAKE THE BANANA: Melt the butter over medium-low heat in a 2-quart fry pan. Stir in the brown sugar and salt. Sauté the banana 3 minutes until caramelized. Flip and caramelize the other side 1 minute. This recipe portions one slice of banana per serving, but make as much banana as you like.

PISTACHIO PANNA COTTA *with* CHOCOLATE MATCHA CRUNCH CLUSTERS

This dessert plays where the crunchy and creamy happily collide. To make the matcha sugar, combine ⅓ cup sugar with 1 teaspoon matcha.

PISTACHIO PANNA COTTA

1 cup pistachios, shelled

2 cups water

Pinch of kosher salt

¾ cups heavy cream

⅓ cup matcha green tea sugar
   (see introductory note)

2 tablespoons agar agar

CHOCOLATE MATCHA CRUNCH CLUSTERS

1 cup rolled oats

¼ cup chopped pistachios, shelled

⅛ teaspoon kosher salt

1 teaspoon matcha green tea powder

1½ tablespoons grapeseed oil or other
   neutral oil

1 tablespoon maple syrup

1 egg white

4 ounces semisweet (64 percent)
   chocolate, chopped (¾ cup)

MAKES 6 TO 8 SERVINGS

TO MAKE THE PANNA COTTA: Soak the pistachios overnight, covered by 2 inches of water. Drain. Blend with the 2 cups fresh water until smooth; you should have 2¼ cups pistachio milk. Strain through a nut-milk bag, cheesecloth, or fine-mesh sieve. Discard the solids. Pour the milk, salt, cream, tea sugar, and agar agar into a 2-quart saucepan. Bring to a boil over high heat. Whisk 5 minutes until the sugar dissolves. Turn off the heat. Grease 8 ramekins and fill almost to the top. Refrigerate 2 hours.

TO MAKE THE CLUSTERS: Preheat the oven to 300°F. Line a 13 by 9-inch sheet pan with parchment paper. Stir the oats with the pistachios and salt. Sprinkle the matcha into another small bowl. Warm the oil and maple syrup for 1 minute in a 2-quart fry pan set over medium-low heat. Pour the oil over the matcha, whisking vigorously for 1 minute. Stir the matcha and egg white into the oats to coat.

Layer the oats in a single layer on the sheet pan. Bake 30 minutes. Cool 1 hour and break into clusters. Line a counter with parchment paper. Stir the chocolate in a 2-quart saucepan set over low heat until melted. Gently stir the clusters into the chocolate to coat. Remove to the parchment paper and cool 8 hours.

Just before serving, top panna cottas with crunch clusters.

CHOCOLATE EARL GREY CUSTARD
with CANDIED KUMQUATS

Chocolate appreciation runs in the family; as a child I discovered that my dad kept a drawer in his bedside table loaded with bars of good chocolate. This custard is inspired by one my dad and I shared at a café by the San Francisco opera house, while discussing what comprises the good life.

CHOCOLATE EARL GREY CUSTARD

2 cups heavy cream

½ cup whole milk

⅓ cup sugar

2 bags Earl Grey tea

5 ounces good semisweet (64 percent) chocolate, chopped (1 cup)

6 egg yolks

CANDIED KUMQUATS

1 cup sugar

8 kumquats, rinsed, seeded, and sliced

MAKES 8 (4-OUNCE) JELLY JARS OR 6 RAMEKINS

TO MAKE THE CUSTARD: Set out 8 jelly jars or 6 ramekins. Preheat the oven to 300°F. Whisk the cream, milk, and sugar together in a 2-quart saucepan over medium heat until the sugar dissolves and it begins to simmer. Turn off the heat. Plunge in the tea bags and twirl the tags around the handle of the pot. Steep 30 minutes. Press on the bags to extract all the steeped liquid; discard the bags. Bring the saucepan to a simmer. Whisk the chocolate into the hot cream.

In a medium bowl, whisk the yolks and gradually whisk the cream in until combined. Strain through a fine-mesh sieve; discard any solids. Fill the jars halfway. Place the jars into a 9 by 13-inch cake pan. Pour 6 cups of water into the cake pan. Cover the pan with aluminum foil. Bake 1 hour and 10 minutes, or until the custard is set around the edges with a bit of jiggle in the middle. Remove the jars and cool to room temperature. Cover and refrigerate for 2 hours or more.

TO MAKE THE KUMQUATS: Cook the sugar and ½ cup water in a 2-quart saucepan over high heat 3 minutes, stirring occasionally until the sugar dissolves. Boil 2 cups water in another saucepan. Submerge the kumquats for 1 minute. Drain. Add 2 new cups of water to the saucepan. Submerge the kumquats for 1 minute. Drain. Steep the kumquats in the sugar syrup for 15 minutes. Drain. Dry on parchment paper. Top custards with candied kumquats.

SALTED ALMOND ICE CREAM *with* MASALA MAGIC SAUCE

Anytime I'm in Austin I find myself at the Gonzo food truck, sipping a Honey Pie Milkshake. The salty sweetness of this ice cream is a nod to that shake, while the shell of spiced chocolate makes this an adult version of dipped cones from the childhood ice cream truck. Magic!

SALTED ALMOND ICE CREAM

2 cups heavy cream

1 cup whole milk

½ cup sugar

2 tablespoons raw honey

½ cup natural almond butter, stirred well

¼ teaspoon kosher salt

MASALA MAGIC SAUCE

1 heaping teaspoon loose masala chai tea, finely ground

3 ounces bittersweet (70 percent) chocolate, chopped (½ cup)

4 ounces semisweet (64 percent) chocolate, chopped (¾ cup)

2 tablespoons coconut oil

MAKES 4 TO 6 SERVINGS

TO MAKE THE ICE CREAM: Stir the cream, milk, sugar, and honey in a 2-quart saucepan over low heat until the sugar dissolves, about 9 minutes. Midway through, stir in the almond butter and salt to an even tawny color. Strain through a fine-mesh sieve into a bowl. Cover and refrigerate overnight. Pour the chilled cream into the ice cream machine receptacle and follow the manufacturer's instructions. Once the ice cream is done churning, freeze at least 2 hours before serving.

TO MAKE THE SAUCE: In a 2-quart saucepan, stir the chai, chocolates, and oil over low heat until melted. Cool 10 minutes before serving. Refrigerate extra sauce in a glass jar. Reheat by submerging the jar in warm water.

CHAI FROZEN HOT CHOCOLATE MALTS

People survive Texas summers one of two ways: swimming pools or ice cream. I spent them in my friend Kathi's pool. This is a tribute to those summers and Kathi's discovery of frozen hot chocolate in New York City, which changed both of our lives.

6 ounces semisweet (64 percent) chocolate, finely chopped (1 heaping cup)

2 cups whole milk

1 cup heavy cream

3 bags or 1½ tablespoons loose masala chai tea

¾ cup masala chai tea, brewed and cooled (1 bag or 1 teaspoon loose), frozen in 6 cubes

8 ice cubes

2 tablespoons malt (optional)

MAKES 4 SERVINGS

Place the chocolate in a large bowl. Bring the milk and cream to a slow boil over medium heat in a 2-quart saucepan. Once bubbles start erupting beneath the surface, turn off the heat. Twirl the tea tags around the pot handle or add the leaves, plunging them into the cream. Steep for 15 minutes. Press on the bags or leaves to extract all steeped liquid; discard the bags or leaves.

Heat the chai cream for 3 minutes over medium heat. Turn off the heat. Pour the cream into the chocolate in three batches, whisking constantly until combined. Cover and refrigerate for 8 hours or overnight, until cold. (Now is also a good time to freeze the masala chai cubes.)

Blend the chilled hot chocolate with 6 chai ice cubes, 8 ice cubes, and malt (if using) until smooth. Serve immediately.

MATCHA TEAFFOGATO *with* TOASTED COCONUT ICE CREAM

Traditionally, an affogato consists of a shot of espresso poured over a scoop of ice cream. Matcha green tea inspired this dramatic deviation. Coconut cream is as different from coconut milk as heavy whipping cream is from whole milk. It can be found in the Asian or Latin American grocery aisles. I use the Chaokoh brand to great success.

1 (13½-ounce) can coconut cream (2 cups)

1 cup heavy cream

½ teaspoon kosher salt

½ cup sugar

4 egg yolks

2 tablespoons thick-cut toasted coconut flakes

2 teaspoons matcha green tea powder

2 cups 175°F water

MAKES 8 SERVINGS

Scald the coconut cream about 3 minutes in a 2-quart saucepan over high heat. Don't stir just yet; it will begin bubbling animatedly and might spurt. Stir in the heavy cream, salt, and sugar and keep on high heat until it begins almost frothing over the saucepan. Turn the heat down to medium low and cook 2 minutes, stirring. Turn off the heat.

Whisk the yolks in a mixing bowl. Gradually pour in the coconut cream, whisking constantly. Strain through a fine-mesh sieve placed over a small bowl. Pour the strained custard back into the saucepan. Cook over medium low until it reaches 170°F. Pour into a bowl. Cover and refrigerate for 24 hours, or until cold. Pour the custard into the cold ice cream machine receptacle. Follow the manufacturer's instructions. Sprinkle in the coconut flakes after the ice cream starts thickening. Churn 3 more minutes. Freeze at least 2 hours before serving.

TO ASSEMBLE: Sprinkle the matcha into a large bowl and vigorously whisk in the water, starting with ¼ cup for 1 minute. Once the tea is clump-free, add more water while whisking until all the water has been incorporated. Scoop one ball ice cream into each bowl. Pour ¼ cup matcha over each. Serve immediately.

TOASTED PECAN PALETAS

Paletas remind me of neighborhood stores we frequented during summer visits to family in Mexico. My favorite was creamy *Paletas de Nuez* (Pecan Popsicles). Here, brisk lapsang souchong tea provides a hint of smoke to the sweetness of maple, pecans, and cream.

½ cup whole milk

2 cups heavy cream

½ cup water

3 tablespoons maple syrup

Pinch of ground cinnamon

Pinch of kosher salt

2 bags or 1 tablespoon loose lapsang souchong tea

⅓ cup toasted, chopped pecans

MAKES 8 TO 10 POPSICLES

Pour the milk, cream, and water into a 2-quart saucepan placed over low heat. Stir in the maple syrup, cinnamon, and salt with a wooden spoon. Stir occasionally until small bubbles form on the sides, about 8 minutes. Turn off the heat and plunge in the tea bags or leaves. Steep for 5 minutes. Press on the bags or leaves to extract all the steeped liquid; discard the bags or leaves. Pour the tea cream into a bowl. Cover and refrigerate until cold, about 3 hours. Remove from refrigerator and stir in the pecans. Carefully ladle into popsicle molds, making sure to get pecans into each. Freeze about an hour and then insert popsicle sticks. Freeze 3 hours more or longer.

HARD CIDER FLOATS *with* MAPLE CHAI ICE CREAM

This adult float is like deconstructed apple pie . . . with a kick. Luscious cream, maple, and warm spices pair perfectly with a dry pear cider like Christian de Druin. If you prefer apple ciders, go with a dry one like Clos du Normand.

MAPLE CHAI ICE CREAM

2 cups heavy cream

1 cup whole milk

½ cup maple syrup

½ teaspoon kosher salt

3 bags or 3 teaspoons loose masala chai tea

2 egg yolks

750 ml bottle hard cider

MAKES 4 SERVINGS

Heat the cream, milk, maple syrup, and salt in a medium-sized pot over medium heat, stirring until it reaches 212°F. Turn off the heat. Plunge the chai bags into the hot maple cream with a wooden spoon. Steep for 30 minutes, twirling the tea strings around the pot handle. Heat the chai cream until warm again. Press on the chai bags with the spoon to extract all steeped liquid. Discard the bags.

Whisk the egg yolks in a medium-sized bowl. Slowly add the warm chai cream in batches, through a fine-mesh sieve, whisking as you pour. Position the sieve over a smaller bowl and strain the chai custard cream again. Cover and refrigerate for 24 hours. Freeze the ice cream machine bowl for 24 hours.

Pour the ice cream custard into the ice cream machine bowl and follow manufacturer's instructions. Freeze for 2 hours before serving.

For each serving, drop 2 scoops of ice cream in a tall glass. Pour in 1 cup hard cider and serve immediately.

JASMINE TEA EXTRACT

Did you know you can easily make your own tea extract? The only ingredients are tea, vodka, and time. I use them in many *Steeped* recipes, but they are endlessly versatile. Extract ideas from your own imagination and get busy infusing!

½ cup loose jasmine green tea

¾ cup vodka

MAKES ¾ CUP

Place the jasmine leaves in a pint-sized glass jar. Pour the vodka over in a swirling motion. Store the sealed jar in a dark, cool place for one month. Strain through a fine-mesh sieve into a clean half-pint glass jar, pressing on the leaves to extract all the steeped liquid; discard the leaves. Store the tea extract wherever you store your vanilla extract.

OTHER FLAVOR EXTRACTS:
EARL GREY, ENGLISH BREAKFAST, *and* MASALA CHAI

Use the method above, but in place of the jasmine tea, substitute ¼ cup from loose or from 8 bags (cut open) Earl Grey, English breakfast, or masala chai.

BITTERSWEET MOROCCAN MINT TRUFFLES

As my last bite to you, I present Moroccan mint *mignardises* laced with lime powder. Tuck them in parchment packets and into the hands of departing dinner guests as a sweet remembrance. I used Rishi Moroccan mint green tea for a pop of peppermint. To make the Lime Powder: Skin 4 limes with a vegetable peeler. Dry the zests until crisp in a dehydrator or 175°F oven for 2 hours. Cool before grinding to powder.

8 ounces bittersweet (70 percent) chocolate, chopped (1½ cups)

½ cup heavy cream

2 tablespoons loose Moroccan mint green tea

⅛ teaspoon Lime Powder (see introductory note)

2 tablespoons good-quality cocoa powder

MAKES 36 TRUFFLES

Line a 9 by 5-inch loaf pan with parchment paper. Pour the cream into a 1½-quart saucepan over low heat. When bubbles begin breaking out on the surface, turn off the heat, and stir in the tea. Steep for 20 minutes. Strain the infused mint cream through a fine-mesh sieve. Press on the leaves to extract all the steeped liquid; discard the leaves.

Place the chocolate into the top of a double boiler or a small stainless-steel bowl and pour in the tea cream. Fill the bottom of the double boiler or a 2-quart saucepan a quarter with water and position the top of the double boiler or the stainless-steel bowl over the water. Set the heat to low. Stir the chocolate cream until melted and combined. Take off the heat and stir in the lime powder.

Spoon the chocolate into the prepared loaf pan, spreading into the corners. Cool 30 minutes. Cover and refrigerate for 2 hours. Line a 13 by 9-inch Pyrex baking pan or sheet pan with parchment paper. Measure the cocoa powder into a small bowl. Remove the loaf pan from the refrigerator. Pull up on the ends of the parchment paper to lift out the hardened ganache. Slice into 36 cubes. Tumble each cube in the cocoa to coat. Place the truffles into the parchment-lined pan, cover, and keep chilled until serving.

RECIPES *by* TEA *and* TISANE

Green Tea Vinegar, 42

Hurricane Popcorn with Tea Furikake, 54

Tea Crackers with Herbed Labneh, 55

Creamy Broccoli Soup, 64

Green Tea Stock, 86

JASMINE

Ginger-Mango Green Tea Smoothie, 16

Orange-Jasmine Brussels Sprouts, 69

Jasmine Cacao Nib Meringues, 95

Spelt Shortcakes with Cantaloupe and
Jasmine Whipped Cream, 98

Jasmine Tea Extract, 112

MOROCCAN MINT

Summer Squash Gruyère Quiche, 33

Creamy Cucumber Roll-Ups, 47

French Lentil, Carrot Curl, and
Moroccan Mint Sauce Tea Toast, 51

Tea Crackers with Herbed Labneh, 55

Mint Pea Soup, 63

Bittersweet Moroccan Mint Truffles, 113

MATCHA

Matcha Chia Pudding Parfaits, 13

Green Tea Egg Wraps Stuffed with
Artichoke Cream and Squash, 30

Green Tea Guacamole with
Grapefruit Tea Toast, 48

Green Tea Coconut Rice, 71

Black Bean Burgers with
Green Tea Basil Aïoli, 78

Green Tea Noodles in Asparagus Sauce
with Goat Cheese Pearls, 82

Green Tea Sesame Shortbread Cookies, 91

Pistachio Panna Cotta with Chocolate
Matcha Crunch Clusters, 103

Matcha Teaffogato with Toasted Coconut
Ice Cream, 108

CHAMOMILE

Chamomile Lassi, 17

Strawberry Chamomile Jam, 21

Oat Pancakes with Chamomile-Scented
Strawberries, Spiked Crème Fraîche,
and Lemon Curd, 25

Chamomile Corn Chowder, 66

Chamomile Risotto with Currants, 89

Chamomile Buttermilk Pudding with
Caramelized Banana, 102

ROOIBOS

Blueberry Scones with Rooibos Honey Butter, 3

Cranberry-Coconut Rooibos Oat Porridge, 10

Buddha's Hand Rooibos Marmalade, 22

Pumpkin Carrot Soup, 68

Rooibos Red Fruit Kanten, 101

TEA PROVISIONS
and GIFTS

TEA EXTRACTS
Earl Grey Tea Extract, 112

English Breakfast Extract, 112

Jasmine Tea Extract, 112

Masala Chai Extract, 112

TEA HONEY
Lapsang Honey, 50

TEA PECANS
Masala Chai Maple Pecans, 35

TEA SALT
Lapsang Souchong Salt, 52

TEA SPICES
Smoky Spice, 28

Tea Furikake, 54

TEA SUGAR
Chamomile Sugar, 27

English Breakfast Sugar, 92

Masala Chai Sugar, 92

Matcha Sugar, 103

TEA VINEGAR
Green Tea Vinegar, 42

RESOURCES

It is impossible to list every tea company, so I've stuck with brands that can be easily procured at specialty or natural grocery stores in the United States. Most of the companies listed under loose teas sell whole leaf tea bags, but for the purpose of cooking, it is more economical to purchase their loose teas instead.

WHOLE-LEAF LOOSE TEAS

Adagio Teas: www.adagio.com

Argo Tea: www.argoteastore.com

DAVIDsTEA: www.davidstea.com

Fortnum & Mason: www.fortnumandmason.com

Harney & Sons: www.harney.com

Ito En: www.itoen.com

Mariage Frères: www.mariagefreres.com

Mighty Leaf Tea: www.mightyleaf.com

Peet's Coffee & Tea: www.peets.com

Rishi: www.rishi-tea.com

Silk Road Teas: www.silkroadteas.com

Steven Smith Teamaker: www.smithtea.com

Teavana: www.teavana.com

The Tao of Tea: www.taooftea.com

Zhena's Gypsy Teas: www.zhenas.com

BAGGED TEAS

Allegro Coffee & Tea: www.allegrocoffee.com

Bigelow: www.bigelowtea.com

Choice Organic Teas: www.choiceorganicteas.com

Numi Organic Teas: www.numitea.com

Paromi: www.paromi.com

Taylors of Harrogate: www.taylorsofharrogate.com

Tazo: www.tazo.com

The Republic of Tea: www.republicoftea.com

Twinings: www.twiningsusa.com

TEAWARE

Breville: electric tea kettles • www.brevilleusa.com

Bodum: teapots and infusers • www.bodum.com

Bonjour: teapots and kettles www.bonjourproducts.com

Chantal: tea kettles • www.chantal.com

Forlife: teapots, single brew cups, iced tea pitchers • www.forlifedesign.com

OXO: fine-mesh sieves, thermometers www.oxo.com

Zojirushi: electric kettles • www.zojirushi.com

ACKNOWLEDGMENTS

Every child should be born to parents who prod them to pursue their passions. I am grateful for my mom and dad's friendship, support, and the love of family, near and far.

Sometimes you need a kick in the pants to get started. I'm so glad that kick came gently from Jeffrey Elliott. To Amy Collins, whose tenacity and belief in *Steeped* found it the right home, thanks for your hard work, tenacity and encouragement along the way. To Grace Suh, thank you for being an incredible editor. Your enthusiasm for *Steeped* rivals my own. To Kirsty Melville, Julie Barnes, Maureen Sullivan, Carol Coe, and the entire team at Andrews McMeel, you create exquisite books that tell important stories through food. Thanks for getting steeped with me. Stephanie Shih, thanks for capturing the light and spirit of *Steeped*. I'm so glad we embarked on this journey together.

Words cannot adequately express my gratitude for my writing mentors: David McHam, Jack Myers, Bruce Levy, Alicia Ostriker, Jeff Friedman, Ilya Kaminsky, and Paula McLain. Every writer should have a keen copyeditor like Katie Wilson—thank you!

To my TEAchers, thank you for sharing your tea expertise and love of the leaf. To Jill Portman and Gary Shinner, who poured their insights into a young graduate not knowing how deeply she would get steeped, thank you. To Joane Filler-Varty for her mentorship in hospitality, creativity in tea kinship, and for being my first reader, *merci*. Thanks to Amanda Sonenberg and Charlie Woodruff for sharing camaraderie and intellect to broaden my tea understanding. Additional thanks go to my second reader, Robert Guiler, as well as Masa Fujii, Jackson Chin, John Simmons, Molly O'Neill, and Ned Heagerty for their support.

To my recipe testers whose insights, thoughtful feedback, and electric enthusiasm provided the necessary bits of detail to make this book ready for home cooks around the world, I thank you personally: Yvonne Hyatt, Katy Daniel, Abby Breedt, Sharona Selby, Sara Ko, Alex Paz, Dominic Green, Dorinda Wegener, Lisa Nelson, Kelda Reimers, Amy Shroads, Catherine Nichols, Routh Barker, Lauren Townsend, Angela Petersen, Vicki Petersen, Meridy Roberts, Alyssa Robinowitz, Bethany Gaudet, Bubba Futerfas, Ben Hyatt, Yesica Arredondo, Julia Smith, Sara Hyatt, Mercedes Harness, Tiffany Flaming, Faith Peralta, Jennifer Griggs, Tanya Welch, Janet Goodman, Anastasia Panagakos, Adrian Conway, Alicia Carlson, Ariel Jutkowitz, Jessica Stroope, and Kresten Froistad-Martin. Thanks also to master food preserver, Ernest Miller, for food preserving testing.

And, to my beloved husband, Nathan, my unflagging champion and first taster, who didn't flinch as tea took over every surface of the kitchen—I thank God for you often.

Photo by Yesica Arrendondo

Annelies Zijderveld is a food writer and creator of the literary food blog The Food Poet, selected by *Alimentum* as one of its favorite food blogs. Her passion for working with good food companies started during her eight years heading up marketing at Mighty Leaf Tea. She is the digital media section newsletter editor for the International Association of Culinary Professionals. She holds an MFA in poetry from New England College and is an associate editor of *Poetry International*. Her work has been published in *Curator, Art House America, Darling* magazine, and *Sated*. She lives in San Francisco with her husband and their pet sourdough starter, Salvatore.

Follow her escapades:
• Pinterest.com/anneliesz
• Instagram.com/anneliesz
• Twitter/anneliesz

METRIC CONVERSIONS *and* EQUIVALENTS

TO CONVERT	MULTIPLY	TO CONVERT	MULTIPLY
Ounces to grams	Ounces by 28.35	Cups to milliliters	Cups by 236.59
Pounds to kilograms	Pounds by .454	Cups to liters	Cups by .236
Teaspoons to milliliters	Teaspoons by 4.93	Pints to liters	Pints by .473
Tablespoons to milliliters	Tablespoons by 14.79	Quarts to liters	Quarts by .946
Fluid ounces to milliliters	Fluid ounces by 29.57	Gallons to liters	Gallons by 3.785
		Inches to centimeters	Inches by 2.54

APPROXIMATE METRIC EQUIVALENTS

WEIGHT

¼ ounce	7 grams
½ ounce	14 grams
¾ ounce	21 grams
1 ounce	28 grams
1¼ ounces	35 grams
1½ ounces	42.5 grams
1⅔ ounces	45 grams
2 ounces	57 grams
3 ounces	85 grams
4 ounces (¼ pound)	113 grams
5 ounces	142 grams
6 ounces	170 grams
7 ounces	198 grams
8 ounces (½ pound)	227 grams
16 ounces (1 pound)	454 grams
35.25 ounces (2.2 pounds)	1 kilogram

VOLUME

¼ teaspoon	1 milliliter
½ teaspoon	2.5 milliliters
¾ teaspoon	4 milliliters
1 teaspoon	5 milliliters
1¼ teaspoons	6 milliliters
1½ teaspoons	7.5 milliliters
1¾ teaspoons	8.5 milliliters
2 teaspoons	10 milliliters
1 tablespoon (½ fluid ounce)	15 milliliters
2 tablespoons (1 fluid ounce)	30 milliliters
¼ cup	60 milliliters
⅓ cup	80 milliliters
½ cup (4 fluid ounces)	120 milliliters
⅔ cup	160 milliliters
¾ cup	180 milliliters
1 cup (8 fluid ounces)	240 milliliters
1¼ cups	300 milliliters
1½ cups (12 fluid ounces)	360 milliliters
1⅔ cups	400 milliliters
2 cups (1 pint)	460 milliliters
3 cups	700 milliliters
4 cups (1 quart)	0.95 liter
1 quart plus ¼ cup	1 liter
4 quarts (1 gallon)	3.8 liters

LENGTH

⅛ inch	3 millimeters
¼ inch	6 millimeters
½ inch	1¼ centimeters
1 inch	2½ centimeters
2 inches	5 centimeters
2½ inches	6 centimeters
4 inches	10 centimeters
5 inches	13 centimeters
6 inches	15¼ centimeters
12 inches (1 foot)	30 centimeters

OVEN TEMPERATURES

To convert Fahrenheit to Celsius, subtract 32 from Fahrenheit, multiply the result by 5, then divide by 9.

DESCRIPTION	FAHRENHEIT	CELSIUS	BRITISH GAS MARK
Very cool	200°	95°	0
Very cool	225°	110°	¼
Very cool	250°	120°	½
Cool	275°	135°	1
Cool	300°	150°	2
Warm	325°	165°	3
Moderate	350°	175°	4
Moderately hot	375°	190°	5
Fairly hot	400°	200°	6
Hot	425°	220°	7
Very hot	450°	230°	8
Very hot	475°	245°	9

COMMON INGREDIENTS *and* THEIR APPROXIMATE EQUIVALENTS

1 cup uncooked white rice = 185 grams

1 cup all-purpose flour = 140 grams

1 stick butter (4 ounces • ½ cup • 8 tablespoons) = 110 grams

1 cup butter (8 ounces • 2 sticks • 16 tablespoons) = 220 grams

1 cup brown sugar, firmly packed = 225 grams

1 cup granulated sugar = 200 grams

Information compiled from a variety of sources, including *Recipes into Type* by Joan Whitman and Dolores Simon (Newton, MA: Biscuit Books, 2000); *The New Food Lover's Companion* by Sharon Tyler Herbst (Hauppauge, NY: Barron's, 1995); and *Rosemary Brown's Big Kitchen Instruction Book* (Kansas City, MO: Andrews McMeel, 1998).

INDEX

Home, the lamp's circumscribed glow:
Dreaming there with fingers on brow
And looks wandering among loved looks;
The hour of infusions of tea, and closed books;
The sweetness at feeling the evening's conclusion;

—PAUL VERLAINE